cable car

by Christopher Swan

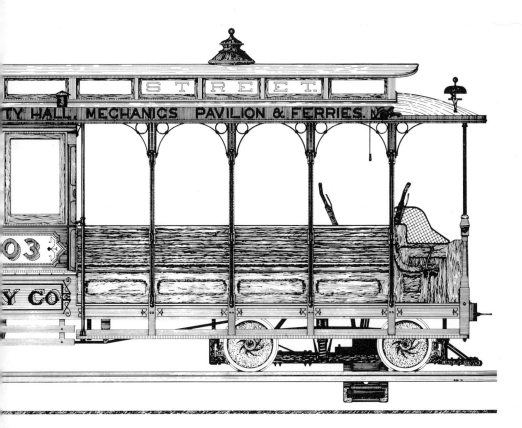

Ten Speed Press

Berkeley, California

CREDIT

Christopher Swan: text of "How it Works" and "As It Could Be," design, photography, drawings and captions. Jeremy Joan Hewes: text of "As It Is," editing and assistance in overall conception. Eileen Douse: text of "As It Was" based on her own comprehensive research. Christopher Burg: aid and cogent skepticism regarding the photographic aspects. Jeffery Moreau: encouragement and many bits of knowledge. Charles Smallwood: all kinds of information, tall stories and much color. Heather Hafleigh of Phil Brown Typography: the setting of type on this, the second edition. Engel Ford of Allert & Bassett: crisp new photostats that make a printed drawing stand out. Howard & Peggy Levine: patience. Phil Wood & Fluffy: friendship and help.

Revisions for the second edition done at the Swan-Levine house in Grass Valley, California.

1⊜
TEN SPEED PRESS
P O Box 7123
Berkeley, California 94707

Library of Congress Catalog Number: 73-77725
ISBN: 0-89815-145-7

Printed in the United States of America

10   9   8   7   6   5   4   3   2

CONTENTS

AS IT IS

HOW IT WORKS

AS IT WAS

as it is

TAKE A LOOK AROUND

The world of San Francisco's cable cars is society in miniature. It is peopled by the men who operate and maintain the system, its passengers and hangers-on and the inevitable splinter groups. Its territory is a city of hills and landmarks, of tourists and their trade. And this small world is prey to all extremes of propaganda and protest, a minimum of crime and violence and its share of suprises.

Three cable car lines currently serve San Francisco: No. 59—Mason-Taylor, which goes through Chinatown and North Beach to Fisherman's Wharf; No. 60—Powell-Hyde, which goes over Nob Hill and Russian Hill to Aquatic Park; and No. 61—California, which runs from the financial district to Van Ness Avenue. Service begins at 6:00 a.m. and continues until 1:00 a.m.; 23 to 31 of the 40 cars are used each day. The fare is 25$^¢$, and transfers are free.

Each year more than 13 million passengers ride this transit system, which comprises 10½ miles of track divided among eight streets. The cable car barn at Washington and Mason streets is the center of this network.

Besides housing the 28 single-ended and 12 double-ended cars still in use, the car barn serves as the powerhouse and maintenance area for the cable railway. The cable winding machinery dominates one floor of the barn; its electric motors, gears and huge wheels drive the four cables at a constant speed of 9½ miles per hour and take up slack as the cables wear. Another section of the barn is a machine shop, where parts are custom made for the aged cars. Mechanics also are on duty at all times to repair broken cable or cope with any other emergency.

In 1967 the cable car barn was opened to the public as combination observation post and museum. Visitors may watch the machinery in operation, inspect early cars and stroll through a pictorial history of San Francisco's cable systems. A plaque on the barn wall identifies the cable cars as a Registered National Historic landmark, an honor bestowed on the system by Stewart Udall, Secretary of the Interior, in 1964.

The cable car system has been recognized in other ways, too. On August 1, 1970—the 97th anniversary of the first cable car run in San Francisco—city officials named the Powell-Market plaza of the Bay Area Rapid Transit system for Andrew S. Hallidie, founder of the cable railway here. The plaza serves as the main entrance to the BART station at the foot of Powell Street, where the cable car turntable is located.

The system is well represented elsewhere, too. A cable grip, valued at $475.000, was sent to the Smithsonian Institution in 1960, and a car from the old Jones Street line was given to Osaka, Japan, San Francisco's sister city. Other "retired" cable cars have been motorized and may be seen traveling trackless streets throughout the city.

Less desirable reminders of the cable cars may be found littering lawns and sidewalks. Some 17 businesses in San Francisco have adopted the cable car name, including a realtor and an advertising agency, restaurants and motels, as well as dry cleaners and haberdashers. Many other businesses simply adorn their bags and boxes with pictures of the cars. The name also appears beyond the city limits—the Cable Car Candy Company (copyright) is located several hundred miles south in Long Beach.

Gripman Al Davison working the track brake on a crowded Bay-Taylor-bound car. The grip lever is released and rests in a blur at the right. As the car ascends the steeper hills the gripman will sometimes have to pull the grip lever back until he is almost horizontal.

The cable cars' small society is manned by only 145 gripmen and conductors, yet the cars carry an average of 35,000 passengers each day. Since the majority of these riders are tourists who apparently haven't time to wait for the next car, working conditions are usually hectic for the crewmen. The crowded cars and hard work take their toll—the turnover in these jobs is almost 100% per year.

As some compensation for his effort, the gripman occupies the only open space on the cable car. He has plenty to do there, though: he operates the grip lever, which engages and disengages the car from the cable, requiring him to exert a force of about 125 pounds each time he pulls the lever all the way back. The gripman also controls a hand brake, foot brake and emergency brake, in addition to ringing rhythms on the car's bell. Gripmen are the objects of many questions and much appreciation, a situation they hardly discourage. Aware of their status, the men often develop elaborate bell-ringing techniques and distinctive styles of maneuvering the grip and brake levers.

Unlike the gripman, the conductor has no sanctuary; he must mingle with the passengers to collect their fares. He directs traffic inside the car, moving riders out of doorways and off steps, calling out stops and cautioning passengers when the car approaches a curve. The conductor operates a rear brake on hills and signals the gripman to start and stop by means of a small bell that he can reach from any point in the car. Although he sees hundreds of faces every day, the conductor seldom overlooks a passenger or asks someone for his fare a second time.

Sometimes the crewmen disagree, which can result in a brief episode of violence on a cable car. As a car was climbing Nob Hill during the rush hour one evening, the gripman did something to the conductor's disliking, so the conductor called his colleague a "birdbrain." The gripman carefully set the car's brakes, then charged the conductor—to the amazement of the vulnerable passengers. Before a policeman could separate them, the scufflers fell on top of a woman passenger, knocking loose some of her teeth.

Tempers have been known to stall traffic in the cable car system, as elsewhere. When a businessman jumped on a moving car once, the gripman hollered at him. The man yelled back, whereupon the gripman stopped the car and ordered the man off. The passenger refused to leave and the gripman refused to budge, stalling ten cable cars and many more autos for half an hour. Finally yielding to the "customer is always right" theory, a Muni inspector relieved the gripman of his duties for the day.

Passengers can also cause chaos on the cars by ignoring the system's rules. A typical problem is the passenger who insists on boarding before the car is off the turntable, which is forbidden because the men can't turn a car while people are swarming for seats. At the Powell-Market turntable one morning, a 71-year-old woman from New York boarded too soon and sat down. When asked to leave, she brandished her cane and said, "It stinks when an elderly girl with a cane can't sit down." Twenty minutes later she got down, reboarded after the car was off the turntable and rode — sitting down — to Fisherman's Wharf. On another occasion, a man picked a fight with the conductor who asked him to wait on board until the car was off the turntable. The passenger hit the conductor in the eye, then fled; service was halted while the conductor was treated at a hospital.

Most of the time, however, crewmen and passengers get along quite well, and the gripmen and conductors often do something gallant or funny or embarrassing. San Francisco Chronicle columnist Herb Caen reports many such incidents: for example, one hot afternoon a gripman had just one passenger. He stopped the car, got off after asking if she would excuse him for a moment, and returned with ice cream cones for himself and the lady rider. A conductor who abandoned his crowded car to use the rest room in a nearby restaurant was suprised to discover that the people had seized power and left him behind. In his absence, a woman tourist complained about the delay, whereupon a local resident pointed to the conductor's bell and said all she had to do was pull that handle twice. She did, and the car moved off, leaving the open-mouthed conductor to chase it up Russian Hill.

Certain rules are made to be interpreted, it seems, such as the policy regarding ice cream on the cable cars. While a gripman even bought his passenger an ice cream cone, one conductor self-righteously expelled four riders from his car for the same "offense." Unfortunately, he didn't recognize two of the four as Lynda Bird and Charles Robb; since Lynda's father was President at the time, the incident made headlines. The visitors took their reprimand graciously, though — and the conductor maintained his anti-ice cream stance even after learning who he had put off. But the city was sufficiently chagrined by all this to send Mrs. Robb a certificate making her an honorary cable car conductor, to which then Mayor Joseph Alioto attached the note, "What flavor was the ice cream!" (butterscotch, no doubt.)

Like many other institutions, the cable car system requires people to adapt to it. In a society increasingly obsessed with speed, cable cars force passenger and motorist alike to accept leisure. The system that has survived a century of unparalleled growth and progress seems to defy speed — or any other modern mania — to kill it.

Its perpetuation is an argument for logic, not for nostalgia. Despite the system's status as a national landmark and the often overzealous attention of tourists and traditionalists, the cable railroad remains a practical means of transportation for San Francisco. It's hard to imagine, for instance, a conventional city bus maneuvering the face of Russian Hill many times each day, starting and stopping for passengers. Yet the cable car does this quietly, without giving off noxious fumes and with relative safety. Indeed, if the public attitude toward the city's cable cars were not so sentimental, and if speed were not the common denominator, it might be possible to consider this form of transit as an alternative to buses and cars in some parts of the city.

This is not to say that the cable car system has no faults. Ideally, the cars run continuously for over 19 hours of each day; in practice, however, they break down rather often. Mechanical difficulties are inevitable in any form of transportation; the cable cars merely have more uncommon problems than a dead battery or an empty gas tank. For example, although the cables are changed every few months (according to how heavily they are used), one of the six cable strands may break and catch in the grip mechanism. If the protruding strand is wider than the maximum grip opening, the car cannot be disengaged from the moving cable and will be dragged along until the cable is turned off at the powerhouse or the car collides with something in its path. On one occasion, a broken strand carried a car into three others waiting to be turned around; all four cars ended up on the turntable and several crewmen were injured.

More serious accidents have resulted from mechanical failures, as well. In 1967 two persons were killed and 30 were injured when a cable car went out of control and plunged down Hyde Street, colliding with an auto near the bottom of the hill. A court later ruled that the gripman of

Leaving Powell and Market for Hyde and Beach. To determine the destination of a Powell car note the colors of the signboards on front and rear. Bay and Taylor is yellow and cream while Hyde and Beach is yellow and maroon.

that car was not responsible for the mishap. A San Francisco court decided a most unusual case regarding a runaway cable car. A woman passenger injured in a 1964 accident sued the Municipal Railway for $500,000, claiming that the psychological trauma of the crash caused her uncontrollable sexual desire. She was awarded $50,000 in a decision that will be a source of both legal precedent and tiresome jokes for some time to come.

Major accidents such as runaway cars are only a small proportion of cable car mishaps, though. More common are minor accidents caused by a passenger's carelessness or a motorist's misjudgement. Occasionally, too, unfamiliarity with the cars breeds panic among riders. As a crowded car started uphill one afternoon the grip mechanism didn't take hold immediately, and the car slid backward a few yards. Fearing the worst, six passengers dove off into Hyde Street, as the car came to a gentle halt behind them.

Unfortunately, the open cars more often inspire riders to show off, engaging in such hazardous practices as leaning out from the running board or failing to hold on. Any injuries resulting from these antics must be judged passenger failures rather than mechanical ones: in short, riders are just as responsible for their actions on the cable cars as anywhere else. So are conductors, as one abruptly learned when he fell off the car on a curve—just after warning his passengers to hold on.

While members of this miniature society could avoid some problems simply by acting sensibly, certain factors are beyond their control. When the streets they travel need repair, one or more of the cable car lines may be shut down. Both the California and Powell-Hyde lines were closed for several weeks in 1970 to allow city crews to repave streets and install sewer lines. The cable system itself also requires maintenance that may affect service. The most recent major adjustment was installation of new cable winding machinery, for which all three lines were closed down for three weeks in 1965.

Like many other subdivisions of the greater society, the cable car system has been the subject of political complaints. San Francisco's Municipal Railway operates the cars at a loss ($2,537,794 in 1970), which prompted the city Public Utilities Commission to recommend shortening the system's hours of service. Citizens' groups protested this action and succeeded in getting a charter amendment on the 1971 ballot. When the votes were tabulated, San Francisco residents had overruled the PUC and amended the city charter to keep service at its present level.

More radical tactics have been used on the cable cars, too. In 1965, 19-year-old Mona Hutchin performed what may have been the first act of the women's liberation movement. The Berkeley coed boarded a cable car at Powell and Market and stood on the steps, in defiance of the long-standing policy prohibiting women from riding outside the car. Six cars were backed up while she ignored polite requests from crewman and

Car number 516 rolling onto the turntable at Powell and Market on a warm spring afternoon. A local portrait photographer, whose studio is in the street, is just passing through the frame while the usual crowd waits in the background for the cable car to be turned.

The marble columns and brass handrails of the St. Francis Hotel frame disembarking passengers at Geary Street and Powell.

fellow passengers to move inside or get off. Two policemen finally removed the woman and took her to the Hall of Justice, but she was released shortly thereafter. A thorough search of the city ordinances later revealed no law against women riding on the running boards, so Muni officials grudgingly acknowledged that women could ride there "at their own risk."

Certain other cultural phenomena touch this small world, as well. For example, the system has its own "groupies," girls who vie for the attention of crewmen. And in a recent attempt to spread nudity beyond stage and screen, a group of young men and women posed for a naked portrait on a cable car. Knowing that the crew was not likely to welcome them aboard for the stunt, the group wore raincoats and waited at a reasonably isolated stop for the first car of the morning. When the car stopped, the passengers threw off their coats and leaped aboard. The gripman ordered them off in no uncertain terms, but their speedy photographer got his picture.

A cable car also has been the unconventional setting for more conventional events than nude photos. A Los Angeles couple "thought it would be nice" to get married aboard one, so they chartered a California Street car for the occasion. The car was stationary during the ceremony —the gripman was ringbearer—but the wedding party enjoyed a moving reception. Another couple (from St. Louis) did not bother to charter a car for their wedding. Their entourage, complete with minister, photographers and reporters, boarded a Powell-Hyde car at Sutter Street; the minister began the ceremony on Nob Hill and finished on the Aquatic Park Turntable.

In addition to providing the location for other people's dramas, the cable car community stages some special events of its own. Foremost among these is the Cable Car Bell Ringing competition, which has been held more or less annually since 1955. An 1882 law requiring gripmen to sound a warning as the car approaches an intersection started the bell ringing, and it has developed into a fine art among crewmen. Several finalists are chosen to compete in the public festivities, for which a motorized (but authentic) cable car is rolled into Union Square. A panel of leading citizens chooses the winner—dubbed "Ding Dong Dandy"— after each contestant has performed for one minute.

Actually, there are few things that can't be found on the cable cars. Theirs is a full and fascinating world where scenery and population change constantly. This microcosm exists to move people, yet it will not be hurried. Its cars expose their riders to the sights, sounds and smells all around them, and the cable railway is unique to San Francisco, where the sensing is exquisite.

SO GET OFF
AND WALK

San Francisco is known for its sensual delights. Indeed, the city is a sort of rolling feast — panoramic views, sweet and sour smells, exotic tastes and cacophonous sounds, often wrapped in a fog that can almost be touched. (And if there's a sixth sense, this atmosphere bathes it, too.) Unfortunately, though, too many visitors to San Francisco limit their feast to famous restaurants, shops and monuments, seldom seeing the city as it is lived before they came and will go on living without them.

Of course the best way to catch a city while it's living is to sneak up on it. Walking is ideal but not always practical on San Francisco's hills, so the most logical substitute is a slow-moving, quiet, open vehicle — precisely the features of a cable car. And since they are prime tourist territory anyway, cable cars offer a chance to sample the unseen city without leaving the beaten track. (This is not to say that San Franciscans have nothing to learn about their city. Many residents avoid the cable cars because of real or imagined tourist crowds; others ride but don't look. So they can take this tour, say, from 6 to 7 a.m.).

The following pages outline a combined walking-riding trip along the three cable car routes, listing some obvious and some rather obscure sights. Most of these things can be seen from the cars but probably won't be noticed. So get off and walk.

POWELL-HYDE LINE 60 &
POWELL-MASON LINE 59

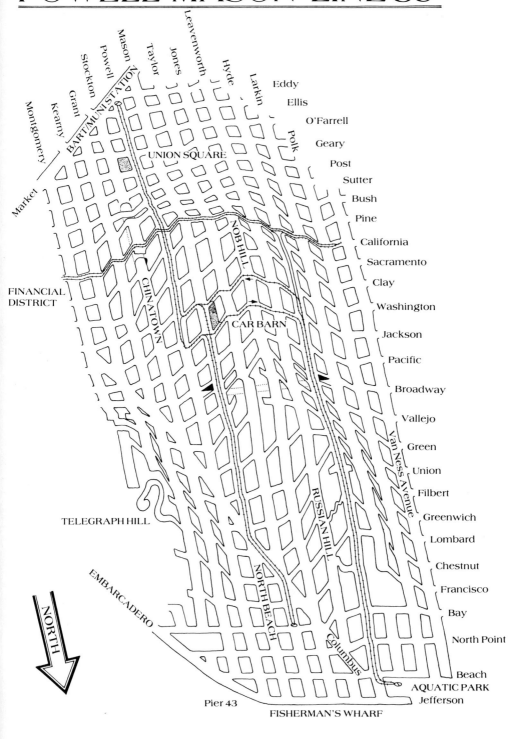

LINE SIXTY

This trip begins at Powell and Market streets, mainly to save the most spectacular till last. (Although Powell is lined with shops and restaurants for several blocks above Market, it is often difficult to board the crowded cars in this area. One solution is to board at the turntable and ride to the top of Nob Hill, then walk down Powell to explore this territory.) After the car has been turned and pushed off the turntable, passengers may board. When it's suitably crowded, the car begins its climb up Nob Hill, an ascent that is easier riding than walking. The car passes Union Square, which—like the city's other parks—is used by the residents. Many well known department stores and specialty shops are located in the Union Square area, as are famous hotels and restaurants.

The crest of Nob Hill is reached at California Street, where the Powell and California cable lines intersect. As the Powell car crosses California, the skyscrapers of the financial district come into view to the east. Moving down the hill, the car enters Chinatown (Grant Avenue, Chinatown's main street, is two blocks to the east). Many old buildings are located in this vicinity, varying from overcrowded apartments to handsome townhouses.

At Jackson Street, the car turns left sharply; holding on is more necessary than usual here. The first intersection on Jackson is Mason Street, where the cable car barn is located one block south at Washington Street. (Cars going the opposite direction use Washington Street and thus pass the barn.) A visit to the car barn is both interesting and essential to understanding how the system works.

Jackson Street is used to return cars to the barn: a car is run up the hill above the yard entrance, switched to a track leading into the yard, the brakes are released and the car shoots down into the yard. As the car continues uphill on Jackson, a backward glance often reveals traffic stalled on the Bay Bridge. The cable car turns right at Hyde Street, passing through a residential section highlighted by hairdressers, greengrocers and a chiropractor who has signs in both Chinese and English. The surroundings change after a few blocks, however, as the car approaches the crest of Russian Hill.

This is a good place to get off and start walking. Conveniently, there is an ice cream store at Union and Hyde to provide energy for the hike. Filbert Street, one block farther along Hyde, provides fine views of Coit Tower on Telegraph Hill to the east and the Presidio to the west. If time and energy permit a longer walk, there are steps down Filbert's hill, then the street goes uphill to Telegraph Hill Park.

Looking northeast from another type of cable car. A glass, outside elevator moves up the east wall of the Fairmont Hotel tower above the corner of Powell and Sacramento streets. Two cable cars are barely visible in this view, one at Clay Street and another near Jackson. Telegraph Hill and Coit Tower are visible in the top center.

A small group of prospective passengers at Powell and Geary. Prospective because by this stop, particularly in the summer, the car has filled to capacity. It's usually easier to board at the Powell and Market turntable.

Looking south down Powell from above Sutter. The Market Street terminous is five blocks distant.

Greenwich Street is at the top of Russian Hill, and on top of Greenwich are the Alice Marble Tennis Courts (just west of Hyde). Everybody sees the Hyde Street slice of the bay, but the tennis courts offer an uncommon, now-you-see-it-now-you-don't view of the whole pie. The Marin hills, Mt. Tamalpais, Angel Island and Alcatraz can be seen through the fence and around the foliage. (Of course the tennis courts are public but their disadvantage is that when a ball goes over the fence, it's gone.) To the west, Greenwich Street also provides a good view of the Palace of Fine Arts.

Lombard Street is next, and it's the occasion for a small lecture. To really "do" San Francisco, it is not necessary to drive down "the crookedest street in the world." Honest. It is infinitely simpler and more considerate of residents to walk down the steps on either side of the crooks. This way, it's possible to see the brick street, the plants that line it and the houses and yards of Russian Hill. Halfway down, Montclair Alley affords a view of Angel Island and Marin's hills to the north.

Still another pleasant side street stroll is Francisco Street, which crosses Hyde two blocks downhill from Lombard. To the east, Francisco is lined with large houses set back from the street, giving a feeling of openness in this heavily populated area. The street curves around to the one below it but appears to end at a retaining wall. Besides affording an intriguing view of the Spanish tower and top of the new addition of the San Francisco Art Institute, this wall is great to lean against and look from.

Looking east from the trees surrounding the Alice Marble Tennis Courts. An in-bound Hyde-Beach car is stopped opposite the crooked portion of Lombard Street.

From Francisco and Leavenworth streets looking east towards Berkeley.

The steep part of Hyde, from Chestnut to Bay streets, may be slippery walking at times; the east sidewalk is slotted for easier going. The open space of Russian Hill Park (on the west side) permits glimpses of the Golden Gate Bridge, Fort Baker and Sausalito. At Bay Street, the environment becomes commercial — import houses, antique shops, restaurants. One block down is North Point Street and the next one is Beach, where the cable car line ends at Gaslight Square in Aquatic Park. This is a cool, breezy place to rest and watch ships, cable cars, people, gulls and dogs, among other things. The Maritime Museum is located at the western end of the park, and the long pier opposite it provides a good look at the wharf area.

With Aquatic Park (free, of course) as a point of departure, the spending can begin in earnest. A block west is Ghirardelli Square, an environmental marvel of shops and restaurants built around the old chocolate factory. Fisherman's Wharf and the Cannery, both jammed with restaurants and shops (not to mention fish markets), spread out to the east of the park.

From Francisco Street looking west with a Hyde car passing in the center. The south tower of the Golden Gate Bridge is visible in the distance.

Helping out on a warm spring afternoon.

Through the Gazebo at Gaslight Square car number 503 is visible being turned on the table. On windy days the gazebo offers a sheltered seat for watching the action.

Aquatic Park end of
Powell/Hyde line center

LINE FIFTY-NINE **59**

The logical return by cable car from Fisherman's Wharf is on Line 59, which ends at Bay and Taylor streets. This route is a variation of the Powell-Hyde line, branching off near the car barn and passing through North Beach. Like the Russian Hill portion of the Hyde Street line, the North Beach and Chinatown sections along this route are best explored on foot.

From the Bay-Taylor turntable the car travels two blocks down Taylor Street, then swings left onto Columbus Avenue. This is part of the City's principal entertainment district, where barkers summon customers to the topless niteclubs, bright lights vie for attention and bars and restaurants offer round-the-clock diversions.

North Beach is also known as a literary and artistic center of San Francisco. The beat generation had its beginnings here, and that tradition is carried on by poets, writers, artists and craftsmen who live and work in this area. While on Columbus Avenue, the car crosses Lombard Street, affording a view of the crookedest street in the world winding up the face of Russian Hill to the west.

The cable car turns right on Mason Street, entering a section of residences and corner stores. Just after the car makes the turn, a glance up Mason reveals the top of the Mark Hopkins in the middle of the street — an illusion provided by the hill, of course. Valparaiso Street, an alley on the west side of Mason, offers a good example of how San Francisco is built. The street's two blocks, which are lined with Mediterranean-style houses (pastel stucco, living quarters above garage), open on a hill solidly covered with buildings. Although the structures are built on several streets at different levels on the hill, from this vantage point it's impossible to tell which building starts where.

Further along, Mason crosses Green and Vallejo streets, where steps extend to the top of Russian Hill through a wooded section. Like many parts of the city, this area contains a mixture of building styles — neat older houses above ivied brick walls at one level, with the upper floors of a modern apartment building above and behind the houses, for instance — all fitted to the terrain. Here, too, the illusion of a building in the middle of Mason Street disappears as the Nob Hill hotels come into full view.

The car continues up Mason to Washington Street, site of the cable car barn. As added incentive for visiting the barn, passengers may get a free transfer when they board the car, get off at the barn, then reboard with the transfer. Beyond the barn, the Mason-Taylor and Powell-Hyde lines merge.

*Water Street, an alley off
Taylor Street, provides a
view west up Russian
Hill. Barely discernible
amongst the walls, roofs,
and trees is the concrete
form of the San Francisco
Art Institute on Chestnut
Street.*

*Bay and Taylor streets late
on a summer evening. A
car is turned as a small
group of passengers
position themselves for
boarding.*

Running up Vallejo
Street from Mason would
be a strenuous task as
there are stairs and paths
for almost two blocks.
Barely visible in this scene
just above the front of the
cable car is a portion of
the stairs, which abruptly
disappear in the thick foliage. At top right a large
apartment building, aptly
named the Summit, caps
Russian Hill.

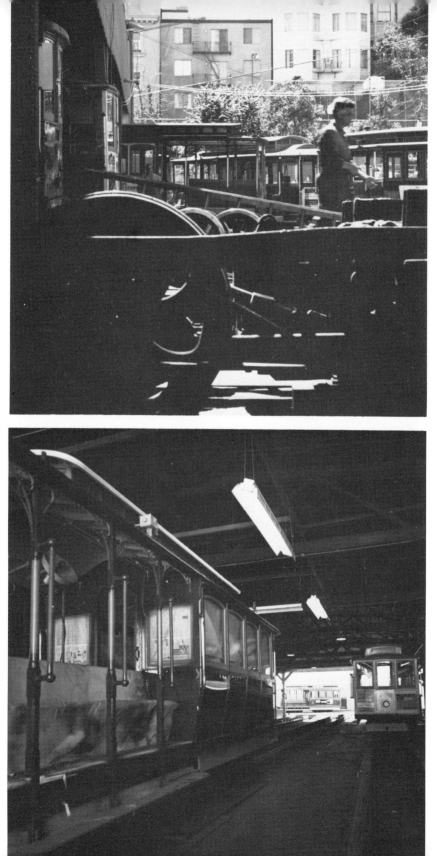

CALIFORNIA STREET
LINE 61

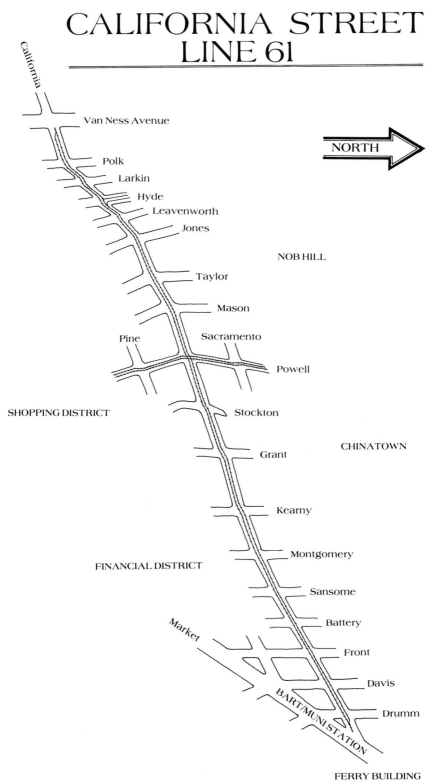

California

Van Ness Avenue

NORTH

Polk

Larkin

Hyde

Leavenworth

Jones

NOB HILL

Taylor

Mason

Pine   Sacramento

Powell

SHOPPING DISTRICT   Stockton

Grant   CHINATOWN

Kearny

Montgomery

FINANCIAL DISTRICT   Sansome

Battery

Market   Front

Davis

BART/MUNI STATION   Drumm

FERRY BUILDING

LINE SIXTY-ONE

The California Street line differs from the two Powell lines in several respects. For instance, these red and brown cars (the Powell cars are green and cream) are double-ended. They have an open section at each end, with the complete grip and brake mechanism between the rows of seats, and a closed seating area in the center of the car. This enables the cars to travel in either direction, eliminating the need for a turntable. Instead, a car is switched to the tracks on the other side of California Street for its return trip. Because they are larger, the California cars hold more passengers (up to 100 when crowded) than the Powell cars, which carry 90 persons when overloaded. Their capacity has its ironic aspect, though, since the California Street cable line is used much less than the two Powell lines.

Although many visitors overlook this part of San Francisco's cable railway, California Street offers a variety of sights and provides access to fascinating places. The line is easy to find, since it crosses the Powell Street lines at the top of Nob Hill (where the switchman controls a special traffic light for the cable cars from a red and brown booth). Because this intersection is the most popular boarding spot on California, it's a good place to start this brief tour.

On the Washington Street side of the car barn a California car is readied for its daily rounds. From this point the car is pushed by hand out of the yard and onto the mainline.

To the west, the car moves downhill gradually, riding the crest of Nob Hill. This area sports hotels, churches and clubs but is increasingly dominated by three-and-four-story apartment buildings. Near the end of this line the car crosses Polk Street, where the assortment of shops and restaurants merits exploration. The western terminal of Line 61 is Van Ness Avenue, commonly called "Auto Row" for its monopoly of automobile dealers in the city. If cable car travel is particularly disagreeable, a passenger can of course visit Auto Row and try his hand (and brake foot) at maneuvering the San Francisco hills. Returning to California and Powell, the cable car descends a steeper side of Nob Hill to the east. The second street crossing California is Grant, the main thoroughfare of Chinatown (Stockton Street passes beneath California in a tunnel). Immortalized by Rogers and Hammerstein, Grant Avenue is a narrow one-way street lined with Oriental shops and restaurants whose reputation for exotic bargains results in a

A Powell car is about to descend Powell Street while a California car at left begins its descent into the financial district.

A California car awaiting passengers at Van Ness Avenue.

perpetual traffic jam. Thus—like so much of San Francisco—the secrets of Chinatown are more likely to be revealed to pedestrians.

Below Grant, the cable car enters a canyon with skyscraper walls—the financial district. This area is dominated by the towering Bank of America building at Kearny Street. At its eastern end, California Street is flat and the buildings lining it are not so tall as those a few blocks west. The line terminates at Market Street, where the Embarcadero Station of the Bay Area Rapid Transit system (BART) is located. The Ferry Building, a landmark of the city's harbor and once the primary embarkation point on the bay, can be seen just to the east of the California line terminal.

When the California Street car reaches the end of the line, the gripman moves to the opposite set of controls and the conductor turns the fare meter back to zero. After pausing a few minutes (the pause is longer on weekends), the rope is taken and the car proceeds back into the canyon.

Looking north from in front of the Mark Hopkins Hotel with the Fairmont Hotel at right. A California car is visible just crossing Mason on its way downtown.

Overlooking California Street from St. Mary's Square. The Hartford building's ground floor facade is visible in the background.

Looking up California Street at Kearny, towards Grant Street and Chinatown. In the center distance is the Fairmont Hotel Tower.

VIEWS

POWELL
AND
MARKET

5

FISHERMANS WHARF
3 BLOCKS
FROM TERMINAL

BAY
AND
TAYLOR

how it
works

Concept: an image in the inventor's mind; mental construction before physical.

Two rails, a center channel, and a passenger car are the major elements. Power the system with large reciprocating steam engines driving sheaves. Keep the cable constantly running; a closed loop through a network of pulleys and tunnels. A device extending down into the channel to grip the cable. Power when you need it — not carried around with you.

Fuel to the boilers, then steam to the cylinders. Long connecting rods begin to move up and down. Sheaves turning until the cable is moving nine point five miles per hour. The steady grind of gears, a reassuring consistency in their sound.

Out on the line a grip wheel is tightened under the arms of a new man: the "gripman." Cable car becomes one with cable.

It worked and still does. The steam engines, original tracks and cars are gone, leaving only a few threads; a brick smokestack over the southwest corner of the car barn at Washington and Mason streets, a few museum pieces within the barn and countless photographs. But even with the changes of time the cable car is still admired as a simple mechanical as well as human solution to a unique problem.

Now the cable car has technological cousins. The elevator and ski-lift both operate on similar principles. The most basic difference between the cable car and its cousins is its ability to connect and disconnect from a constantly moving cable. It should be noted that the elevator is a unique device, as it is the only privately owned form of public transportation that arrives within seconds, travels up to 25 miles per hour, operates automatically and, unless one rents in its building, costs nothing.

Compared to the larger world of transportation the cable car differs in one major way. Like the electric train, with its third rail or overhead wire, cable cars need a medium both to travel upon and to obtain power from. Most railways, buses and automobiles require a medium as support only since their power is self-contained. In contrast, think of the airplane or submarine, which travels within its medium rather than on it.

Within the transportation spectrum the cable car is not only an unusual machine but one composed of vehicle and medium spread over topography. A machine capable of moving, during peak hours, 30 separate vehicles carrying over 1800 people. This amounts to approximately 270 tons. With the help of some gears, 740 horsepower moves all this. Now compare that with the average American automobile placed in the urban condition; up to 300 horsepower propelling only two people! Of course the key in this comparison is how the power is used.

This is not to give the impression that the cable car is mechanically faultless or incredibly efficient, because neither is the case. In fact there are often times when its mechanical faults cause it to be gloriously inefficient, somehow endearing it even more to local residents.

To explain the actual workings of the cable car system its parts are discussed in order of complexity, beginning with the cable itself. Paralleling the text are photographs and drawings to aid this explanation. A few of the drawings are referred to as "sections," which means an imaginary slice through an object as a knife through butter. They are used to expose parts not visible under normal conditions, as the front cover "split section" exposes the construction of the car's body.

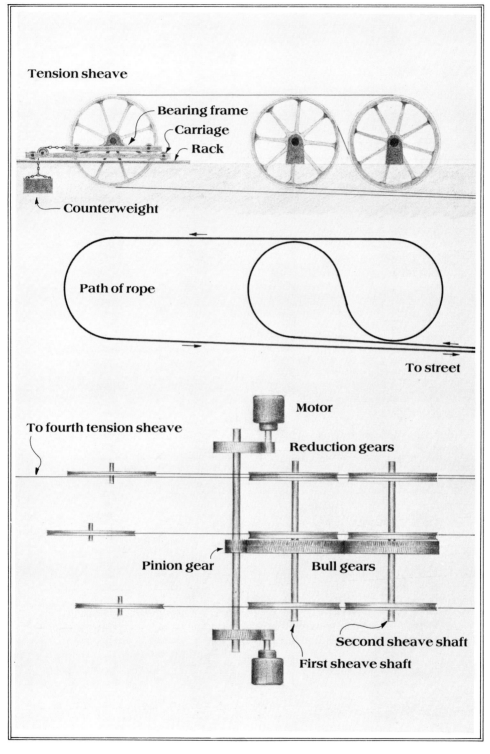

Tension sheave

Bearing frame
Carriage
Rack

Counterweight

Path of rope

To street

Motor

Reduction gears

To fourth tension sheave

Pinion gear

Bull gears

Second sheave shaft

First sheave shaft

CABLE WINDING MACHINERY

Before founding the cable car system, Andrew Hallidie was engaged in the business of providing wire-rope for suspension bridges, mining hoists and related devices. He therefore understood the properties of wire-rope and was able to visualize its role in a cable car system — to say nothing of imagined financial gains. The term "wire-rope," although technically correct, was soon shortened to "rope" for simplicity. One and one-quarter inches in diameter, the rope has a hemp center and steel wrap for two reasons: All steel cable would have considerably less flexibility and would not "give" as much when a load was applied, thus increasing the chance of breakage. Second, rope alone could not withstand the friction from constant contact with the grip's jaws. The combination of the two is therefore a compromise resulting in a wire-rope with the best properties of both materials, giving flexibility in length and cross-section plus more strength and resistance to frictional wear.

Each of the four ropes, Mason, Powell, Hyde and California, is one continuous loop and each passes through the powerhouse at Mason and Washington streets. Within this building are six large sheaves ("sheave" — any grooved wheel or pulley) driven by a single 740-horsepower electric motor. In combination with gears the sheaves act as large levers to multiply the power of the motor.

Connecting the motor and sheaves is a pinion gear riding on a mainshaft. At both ends of the mainshaft are electric motors and reduction gearboxes, one of which is capable of replacing the other in the event of breakdown. Near the center of the mainshaft turns the herringbone pinion gear driving the two "bull" gears. Bull gears, one on each sheave shaft, act to turn the sheaves themselves.

As one set of sheaves is driven by the other they turn in opposite directions. There is a very definite but not noticeable reason for this; coming into the powerhouse from the street the rope passes under the second sheave without contact, then wraps around the first sheave and passes around three-quarters of its surface. Off where the two sheaves are closest. Onto the second sheave and around to the top then straight back to the tension sheave. Having gone half-way around the tension sheave the rope departs and passes in a trough beneath sheaves one and two, then back into the streets. Without the figure-eight pattern around the power sheaves the rope would certainly slip, causing a substantial waste of energy. As it is designed the contra-rotating sheaves act as brakes on one another.

Side view of power sheaves. The tension sheaves are to the left just out of the photograph. At right can be seen the California rope lying on the floor, as this photograph was taken at the same time as the view on the opposite page. The reduction gearbox of the second motor is visible at the far end of the mainshaft.

On the right are the two shorter ropes, the Powell (9,150 ft.) and the Mason (10,150). In the center the Hyde rope (15,700) is visible tied to a railing. At the far left the California rope (21,500) is visible hanging limp from a support pulley. The California and Hyde lines were temporarily shut down when this photograph was taken which also accounts for the stilled tension pulleys in the background. The bull gears are visible, although blurred by motion, left of the center sheaves.

At the rear of the machinery area are three racks which carry the tension sheaves. Each rack is simply a pair of rails separated by a trough. Riding on these rails are four tension sheaves mounted in carriages. Their purpose is to both maintain constant tension on the ropes and take up slack caused by wear. Sustaining tension is accomplished by placing the sheave in a bearing frame so it can travel a short distance within the carriage. There are two large chains connecting the bearing frame to a counterweight suspended from the carriage and contained within the trough. As the counterweight drops, taking up day-to-day wear, the sheave gradually moves back within its carriage. When the sheave has reached its limit, the carriage is moved back until the sheave is again at the front of the carriage and the counterweight is raised. This process continues as a periodic adjustment until the carriage has reached the rear corner of the powerhouse, signaling that the rope is exhausted and will break if not replaced.

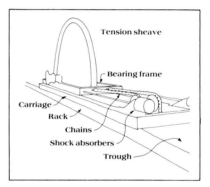

The Mason rope tension pulley with the power sheaves visible in the background. Following the chains around their pulleys locates the counterweight which is hanging just out of view in the trough.

From the tension sheaves the ropes pass beneath the power sheaves and through a series of vaults and tunnels to their various tracks. One tunnel runs beneath Washington Street from Mason to Powell carrying the Mason, Powell and Hyde ropes; another passes beneath Mason Street from Washington to California. The second is a good example of the circuitous route one rope takes: the California ropes runs from the powerhouse up Mason Street to California Street, its tunnel marked only by surface cover plates. Once on California the rope turns west and moves back down the back of Nob Hill to Hyde Street, turning up Hyde to a reversing pulley at Pacific Avenue, then back to California and down to Van Ness Avenue. Reversing again for the eastbound track, the rope proceeds to the Market-Drumm streets terminus, reverses again, and continues up Nob Hill to Mason, where it returns to the powerhouse via the tunnel. The detour up Hyde from California allows California cars to connect with the Hyde line for travel to and from the barn. A switchback between Washington Street and Pacific Avenue allows cars to switch over from one line to another.

TRACK

A major difference between normal railroads and cable lines is the necessity that a cable line's track structure support the rope as well as the car, requiring structure under the rails to maintain the channel, rail gauge, and slot rails in proper orientation to one another. A steel yoke, spaced at regular intervals, carries the rails and forms the shape of the channel. The channel, constructed of brick or concrete, provides space for the rope and grip to pass.

The carrier pulley is the most common of the many pulleys that carry and guide the rope. Spaced approximately 15 feet apart, the carrier pulleys sit at the bottom of the channel, giving the rope a surface to ride on. When a car passes, the rope is momentarily lifted off the pulleys since the grip is about six inches above them. Another type of pulley is the crown pulley, which is located at the top edge of hills; a large wooden or steel hatchcover between the two rails mark its position. The crown pulley's main purpose is to resist the rope's tendency to seek the shortest distance between two points. It is larger than the carrier pulley, since it must take a downward force rather than just the weight of the rope. Other pulleys will be explained later since understanding their use is dependent upon knowledge of other components in the system.

The reconstruction of the crown on California at Stockton Street shows the track structure before it was buried. The slot rails are in place on both tracks, while the support rails have yet to be installed. This particular crown was rebuilt because the original angle was so sharp that automobiles coming down California would, if going more than 25 m.p.h., leave the pavement altogether.

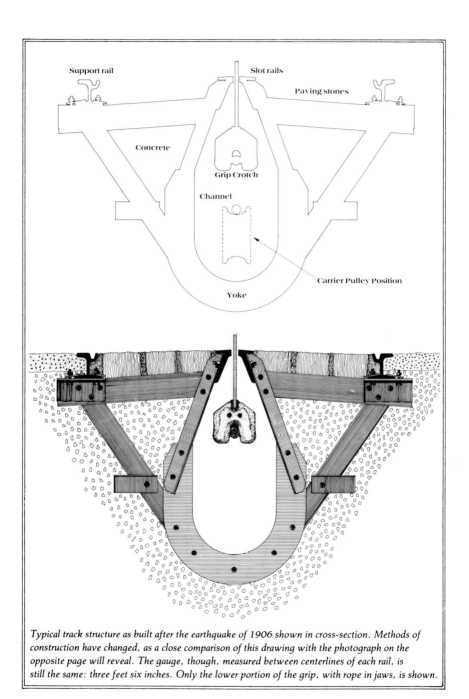

Support rail   Slot rails

Paving stones

Concrete

Grip Crotch

Channel

Carrier Pulley Position

Yoke

Typical track structure as built after the earthquake of 1906 shown in cross-section. Methods of construction have changed, as a close comparison of this drawing with the photograph on the opposite page will reveal. The gauge, though, measured between centerlines of each rail, is still the same: three feet six inches. Only the lower portion of the grip, with rope in jaws, is shown.

CABLE CARS

Basically, both types of cable cars (California and Powell) are composed of the same or similar parts. Trucks, which carry the wheels, support a frame and body constructed mostly of hardwood with steel bracing and side panels. Window frames, doors and similar details vary only slightly in dimension.

The difference between the two types of cars is that one is single-ended and the other is double-ended. California cars, of which there are 12, are double-ended, symmetrical and do not require a turntable to reverse direction. Powell cars, at 27, are more numerous and easily the most thoroughly photographed transit vehicle anywhere. The Powell cars are single-ended and unlike the California type are practically all different. Whereas the California cars were all built around the same time, the Powell cars are products of countless reconstructions and modifications. The most noticeable variation among Powell cars is the roof. They all have what is referred to as a "clerestory," which means the second roof supported by small, openable windows. When cable cars were first constructed the clerestory was included from earlier horsecar designs for ventilation and daylight, as kerosene lamps produced fumes and little light. On cars presently in use there are two types of clerestories; all California and some Powell cars have a simple, straight clerestory, while the other Powell cars have a "Bombay" roof. The Bombay is simply an elaboration of the clerestory with curved top windows in front and rear and a higher center roof. It doesn't accomplish anything more than the simple straight roof but succeeds in demonstrating the coachbuilder's craft.

The cable car is controlled by both gripman and conductor actuating various levers, pedals and bells. At both ends of the California car are duplicate controls consisting of two pedals, three levers, two bells and a light switch. Between the front seats on Powell cars the same conglomeration is grouped, giving the same control with the exception of the conductor's rear platform brake staff.

The three bells may at first seem frivolous but when a crowded car is passing through traffic they are used. Two small bells, above the gripman's station and rear platform, serve as communication between gripman and conductor over the heads of talkative and usually wall-to-wall passengers. Another bell on the roof above the gripman is used to warn of the cable car's presence. This bell is also used by some gripmen to cheer the day by providing musical accompaniment to the normal street noises. Talent is officially rewarded at the annual bell-ringing contest.

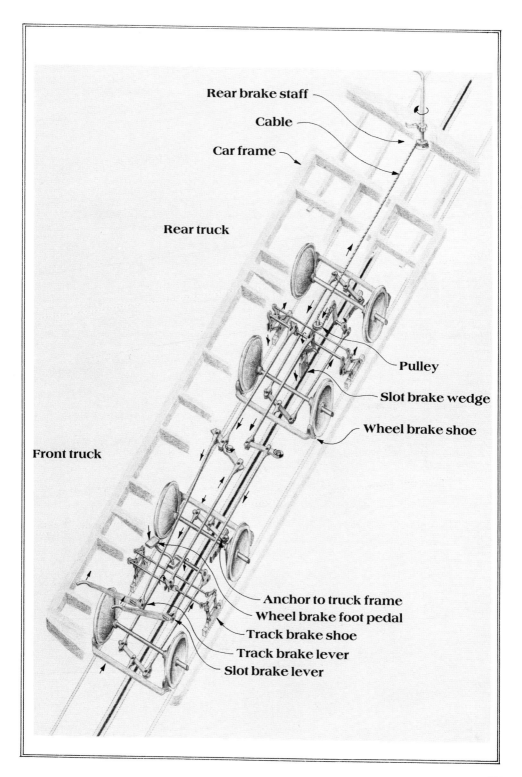

Rear brake staff

Cable

Car frame

Rear truck

Pulley

Slot brake wedge

Wheel brake shoe

Front truck

Anchor to truck frame

Wheel brake foot pedal

Track brake shoe

Track brake lever

Slot brake lever

Most of the time the gripman controls the car; only on the steepest hills does the conductor work the rear brake. The remainder of his time is spent circulating among the passengers collecting fares, giving advice and rubbing shoulders. As he gathers fares he pulls a lever on one of the four rods, which in turn actuates one of the two fare-recording meters located at either end of the car; one is for regular fares, the other for senior citizens, who travel at a reduced rate.

The one light switch previously mentioned triggers the only electricity aboard the cable car. A cluster of batteries beneath the front seats power the headlight, running lights and interior lights. Originally light was provided by kerosene lamps.

Among the controls at the gripman's station are two pedals. The larger operates one of the brake systems, the smaller is used only on wet days when the rails are coated with a lubrication film of water. Pressing this small pedal releases a valve causing sand to be spread on the rails just in front of the wheels. The front wheels then crush the sand, leaving a white powder on the rails and resulting in increased traction and hence greater braking power.

Another rainy day operation was once accomplished by an electric windshield wiper mounted on the front center window. It proved to be a wasteful idea, however, since a day of rain would result in a dead battery. Now, an observant rider may notice evidence of a once common procedure for rainy days—sacks of "Bull Durham" tobacco hanging from a lever on the fare-recording rod above the gripman. Periodically he will

An outbound Hyde car pausing at Jackson and Mason on a winter evening. On a night like this the conductor can enjoy a little peace, for the passengers are not wall to wall. Note the fare recording meter above the doorway.

Close-up of a California type truck. One wheel and half an axle can be seen at top left, while the other axle crosses from bottom center to right center. Parallel to and between both axles is the bolster which connects the two side-frames. In the center of the bolster rests the receptacle for the kingpin, visible as a dish-shaped protrusion at upper left.

wipe the front windows with the damp sack, leaving a thin film of oil that causes the raindrops to roll off the glass.

The cable car is carried by two trucks, each with two axles and four wheels. Until recently there were two types in use, the inside-frame Powell type and outside-frame California type, which are virtually identical in operation. The former is becoming rare simply because its inside frame makes the bearings, which must be lubricated, almost inaccessible. Consequently, the explanation and illustration of the truck shall be restricted to the more common outside-frame California type.

Just beneath the gripman's feet is a kingpin protruding down from the car's frame and mating with a receptacle on the bolster, comprising the only load-bearing connection between the body and wheels. (The "bolster" is the lateral beam in the center of the truck which distributes the load to the two side frames and hence to the wheels.) Constructed of rolled steel and castings, the truck provides a frame for shock absorption, wheels, bearings, grip and brakes. Beneath the bolster are six large springs that absorb shocks from the wheels. From the side there appears to be only one spring, but a close look will reveal two more just behind it. These coils must support anywhere from six tons of empty cable car to ten tons full, which accounts for their massive proportions.

Journal boxes, located on the sides of the truck, contain the bronze bearings in which the axles ride. Each journal supports approximately one eighth of the cable car's weight. The bearings are lubricated by oil-soaked cotton waste packed in the box.

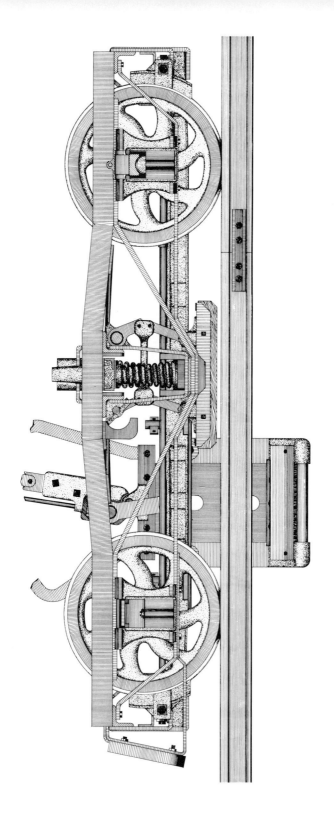

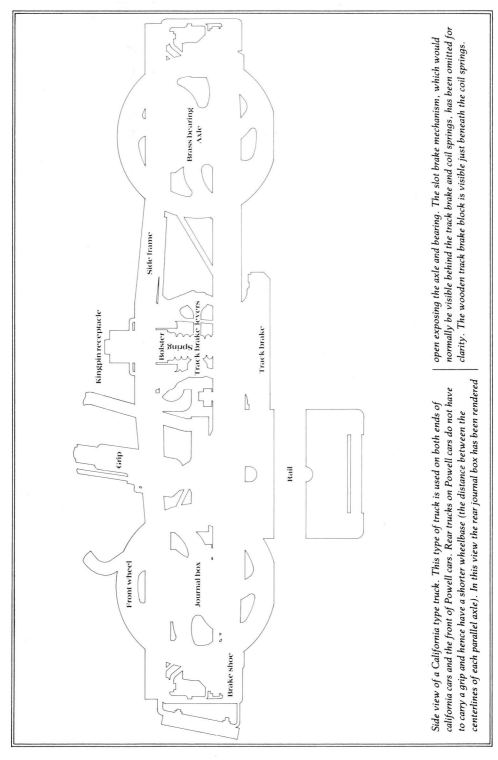

Side view of a California type truck. This type of truck is used on both ends of california cars and the front of Powell cars. Rear trucks on Powell cars do not have to carry a grip and hence have a shorter wheelbase (the distance between the centerlines of each parallel axle). In this view the rear journal box has been rendered open exposing the axle and bearing. The slot brake mechanism, which would normally be visible behind the track brake and coil springs, has been omitted for clarity. The wooden track brake block is visible just beneath the coil springs.

63

Back to the controls: among the assortment of levers and pedals previously mentioned are two brake levers and a pedal. A fourth brake exists in the rope itself; as grip is maintained on the steeper hills, the car is pulled down the hill against its own brakes. Passengers who breathe through their noses will sometimes catch the scent of burning wood, which means the track brakes are is use. When the right-hand lever is pulled four pine blocks, two per truck, are pressed down on the rails and their friction causes the wood to burn slightly. The second brake system is actuated by the large foot pedal at the gripman's station; standing on this pedal presses steel shoes against all four wheels of one truck. On Powell cars the gripman's pedal works the front brake shoes, while the conductor operates the rear platform brake staff controlling the rear shoes. California cars, on the steeper hills, require the conductor to use the pedal and lever opposite from the ones the gripman is using.

Upwards of six tons gathering speed down a steep hill can attain 60 miles per hour if not stopped by brakes or some obstruction. Occasionally the rope is lost, either from carelessness or malfunction, and the cable car does gain too much speed for the normal brakes to be effective. In this rare instance the third brake lever, which is painted red, is pulled. This action drives a steel wedge down into the slot and stops the car quite abruptly. The steel wedge, located on rear Powell car trucks and on both California car trucks, seems primitive but is effective — so effective that it usually must be cut out with an acetylene torch because friction can weld it to the slot rails.

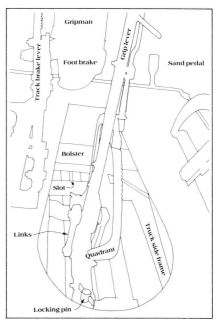

The gripman is shown standing on the brake shoe pedal while the grip is in partial release position and the track brake lever has been pulled. The hole in the floor is large enough to allow for the grips replacement—it must be lifted up through the floor—as well as its meanderings through curves.

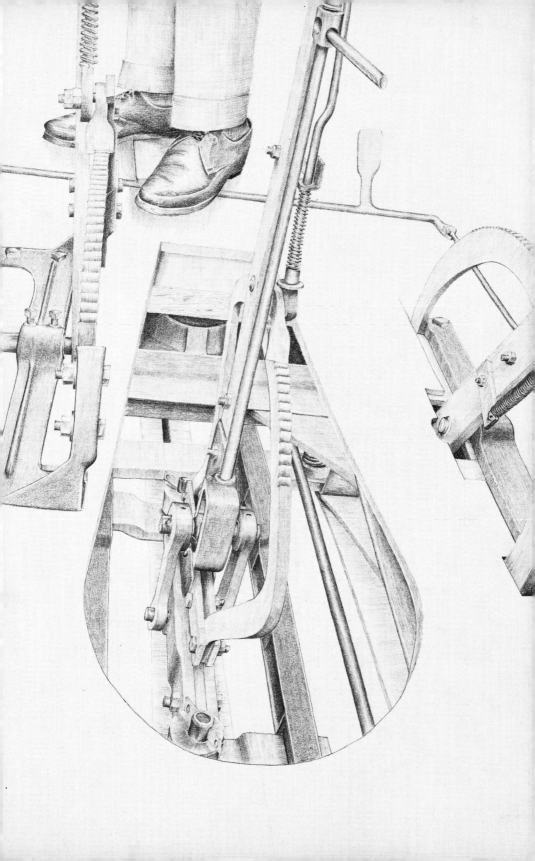

GRIP

"Grip" is a logical term for what is simply a 300-pound pair of pliers. The grip performs the most important function on the cable car and is easily its most complicated single mechanism.

This king-sized pair of pliers can be broken into two components with three possible positions. The first component is composed of the carry-frame, links, shank, crotch, rollers and sand plates. Within these parts functions the second component: grip lever, ratchet release, adjustment rod, pawl, quadrant, center plate, hinges, jaws and dies. In use the first position is full release, in which the grip lever is all the way forward. In this position the center plate is all the way up, the jaws are wide open and the rope is dropped. Second position, just previous to forward movement of the car, is partial release. Viewed from the side, the grip lever is then approximately vertical and the jaws are containing the rope but not gripping it. Usually this is the position when the car is stopped for passengers or traffic. Third position is full grip, which requires most gripmen to pull until they are almost horizontal. This action forces the center plate down, further pushing the jaws against the roller bars and thus closing on the rope. The quadrant and its ratchet allow the gripman to lock the lever in any position while he relaxes his arms or performs other tasks. It should be noted that the three positions mentioned are not accurate as increments on a compass but are "felt" by the gripman. A degree of practice is necessary before a gripman can feel when the gripping point is reached.

Occasionally the passenger will notice the gripman turning the adjustment rod on the grip lever. This is to take up slack in the relationship of various parts caused by wear of the dies. Within the jaws, the dies are the only part of the cable car to actually contact the rope and are therefore frequently replaced.

"Let Go" painted between the rails signals some type of obstruction which the rope and grip must negotiate separately—usually switches or curves. Beyond the obstruction, "Take Rope" is soon visible, indicating the pick-up point. Since the rope normally rides on carrier pulleys below the grip's jaws, two devices are placed in appropriate positions allowing the rope to be regained. A simple depression is usually used to lower the car about six inches so the jaws are around the rope. One such depression is located just west of Mason on California Street where the California rope begins its loop through the powerhouse via Mason Street. Another is visible between Mason and Powell streets on Washington. When cars leave the barn to begin service they roll by gravity down to a switch on Washington Street. Just after passing through the switch the car sinks into a depression to take the Powell rope for the trip downtown. On the return trip up Powell the car must drop the Powell rope at

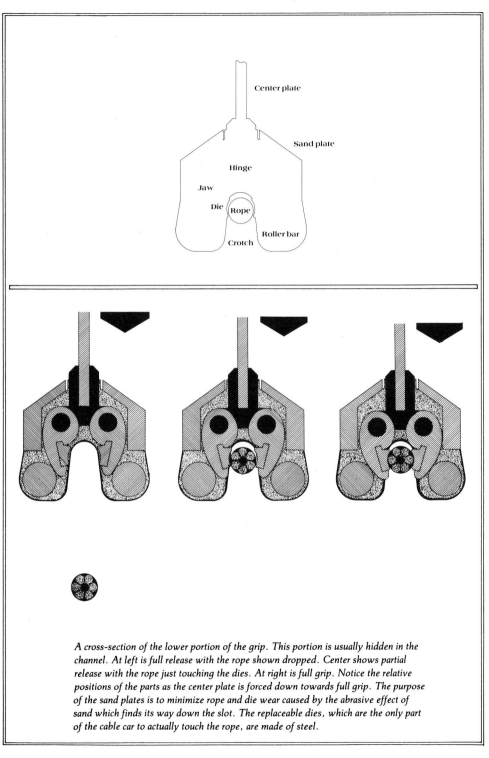

A cross-section of the lower portion of the grip. This portion is usually hidden in the channel. At left is full release with the rope shown dropped. Center shows partial release with the rope just touching the dies. At right is full grip. Notice the relative positions of the parts as the center plate is forced down towards full grip. The purpose of the sand plates is to minimize rope and die wear caused by the abrasive effect of sand which finds its way down the slot. The replaceable dies, which are the only part of the cable car to actually touch the rope, are made of steel.

67

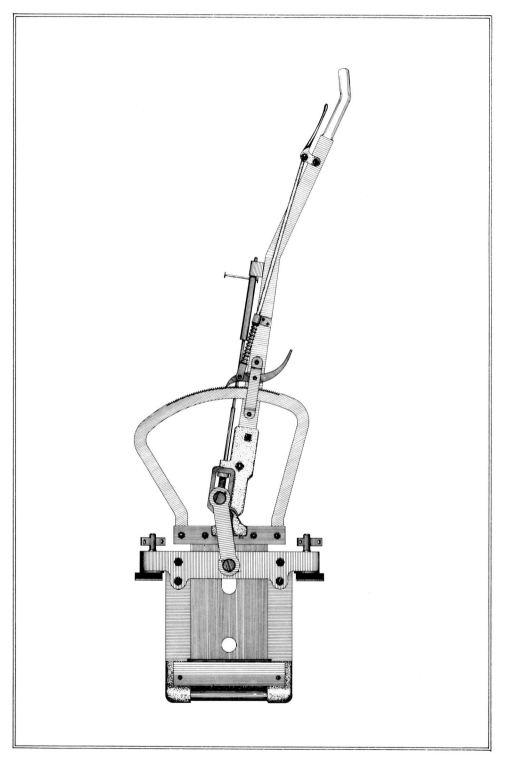

In this side view of the grip the two carry bars are shown in black. These two bars are the only connection between the car and the grip. They rest in a sub-frame within the truck and are capable of moving laterally to allow for variations in the slot. The top bearing of the link is the fulcrum of the grip lever. By adjusting the position of this bearing through the adjustment rod the gripman can change the various parts' relative positions to take up wear of the dies.

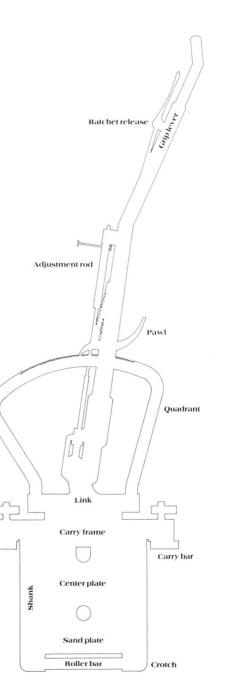

Ratchet release

Grip lever

Adjustment rod

Pawl

Quadrant

Link

Carry frame

Carry bar

Shank

Center plate

Sand plate

Roller bar

Crotch

Car 506 about to depart from Powell and Market from Bay and Taylor. While the conductor pulls the gypsy up the gripman has a hand on the grip lever ready to pull back to partial release as soon as he feels the vibrations of the cable.

California Street and roll three blocks to the switch between Washington and Jackson streets. At this point either the Mason (right) or Hyde (left) track is taken. Just beyond the switch a depression allows one of the two ropes to be gripped.

The second method of regaining the rope is slightly more complicated, since it involves pulleys which actually push the rope up. This device, known as the "gypsy," consists of two pulleys just beneath the rope and connected to a lever in the street. The lever itself is visible within a thin slot paralleling the track. When the rope must be regained the conductor steps down from the car, which is stationary, and lifts up the lever, thus pushing the rope up and between the grip's jaws. As soon as the rope is in the jaws, its movement causes the grip lever to shake, and the gripman draws the lever back to partial release position — containing but not gripping. The conductor then releases the gypsy and jumps aboard. Full grip is gradually applied and the car moves forward...

SWITCHES

On cable railways the act of transferring a car from one track to another is complicated by the existence of the rope and grip. Retaining the rope through a switch would require complicated pulleys and various other underground contrivances. To avoid this added complication almost all switches are located on hills so the car can roll through by gravity, then regain the rope beyond. This method still requires a slot for the grip to pass through and results in a complex tangle of rails and plates. To actuate the switch the conductor pulls a lever in the street that moves a small "point" rail to one side, forcing the wheels to roll through the switch.

The switch on Washington Street below Mason. At upper right can be seen the painted lines which mark the location of both the switch ''point'' and the lever which moves it. Cars travel towards the camera. The left-hand track is the Powell line leading downtown while the right-hand track also leads to Powell but turns north to allow cars to return to the barn.

CURVES

There are two basic types of curves — roll-through and pull-through. Roll-through usually means the car must release the rope and roll through by gravity. This allows the rope to continue straight to a pulley beyond the curve, where it turns 90 degrees, and then is picked up again at the other end of the curve. Pull-through or ascending curves are considerably more complicated, since the rope must move around the curve as the grip does. This is accomplished by a series of closely spaced horizontal pulleys on which the rope rides. Above the pulleys and closer to the slot is a chafing bar, which acts as a brace to prevent the grip from being bent sideways by the pull of the rope. This is the first thing the grip strikes when entering the curve. As it passes through, the rope is lifted off, then returned to the pulleys. Entering this type of curve a passenger can notice the change in the grip lever's movements caused by the crotch striking the chafing bar then following the bar's slight undulations.

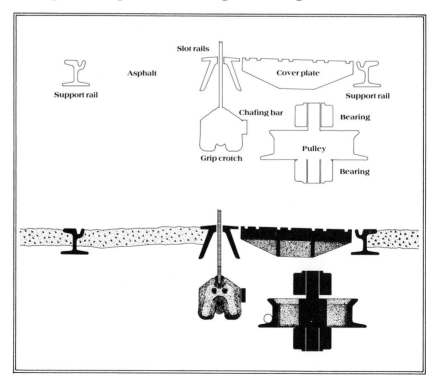

TURNTABLES & SWITCHBACKS

Each of the three turntables, Powell-Market, Bay-Taylor and Hyde-Beach, requires the cable car to roll on by gravity or inertia. At Market the car stops 50 feet from the table, unloads passengers, then moves forward until a "let go" point is reached, where the rope is dropped and the car rolls through the short curve by inertia and onto the table. Under the turntable is a short tunnel where the rope passes to a reversing pulley on the other side. After the car is turned it is pushed off the table and into a depression, where the rope is regained for the climb up Powell. Both the Bay-Taylor and Hyde-Beach tables are similar in use with two exceptions: Bay-Taylor uses a gypsy to regain the rope and Hyde-Beach requires cars to roll on by gravity rather than inertia.

Since they are double-ended, California cars do not require a turntable to change direction. Consequently a switchback simply allows the car to roll onto the opposite track. For example, upon reaching Van Ness Avenue the car proceeds past the switch to the end of track and the rope is dropped. The conductor then throws the switch, whereupon the gripman releases the brake, causing the car to roll onto the opposite track, where the rope is taken by gypsy for the eastbound trip. At the Market Street end the operation is similar except that the car rolls through the switch by inertia and the rope is dropped just before the switch is entered.

Looking into the Bay-Taylor turntable pit. Note the pulleys, one at left and another at right next to a small hole. Both act to guide the rope beneath the turntable mechanism to a reversing pulley out of the photograph to the right. The turntable is shown on the opposite page. At the time both photographs were taken the turntable was being rebuilt with new surface decking.

CROSSINGS

Probably the most complicated piece of trackwork is the crossing at Powell and California streets. Two tracks crossing two others are not unusual on normal railroads, but add four constantly moving ropes, hills on all sides, plus automobile traffic and complications just develop. Consider the four ropes. Two must pass above the other two, meaning one of the lines cannot retain the rope through the crossing. Since the California line was there first, the Powell line had to devise a method of crossing the California rails. Luckily, California Street is wider than Powell so cars can release the rope, roll across and regain it on the other side, whereas California cars can maintain full grip through the crossing and stop only on the west side.

A Powell car approaching California from Market Street waits one block below California (Pine Street) for a green signal. Operated by the crossing guard, the signal tells the Powell gripman that the intersection will be clear of California cars and other Powell cars in his path. The gripman then begins the ascent. Just after he crests the hill there is a slight depression, where the rope is dropped and the car rolls by inertia across the California tracks. In case he must drop the rope too soon because of obstructing automobiles, a safety latch located just below the crest prevents the car from rolling back down the hill, although this situation is rare. Proceeding north by gravity past Sacramento, Clay and Washington streets, the car does not regain the rope until passing the Powell-Jackson switch.

Beneath the rails a number of devices carry the Powell rope under the California line and protect both from damage. Four pulleys, fixed over the Powell rope two to a side, hold it beneath the California rope. As a Powell car approaches the gripman must drop the rope soon enough or an alarm will sound, warning him to drop it immediately. If he doesn't heed the warning a steel bar will obstruct further upward passage of the rope, causing it to be literally torn from the grip's jaws — damaging both. This may sound brutal but it's simply insurance, because continued forward movement would either damage the pulleys or their position would tear the rope from the jaws at such an angle as to probably cut the rope. It is also considered easier to repair the rope and one grip than to tear up a crossing, halting all service.

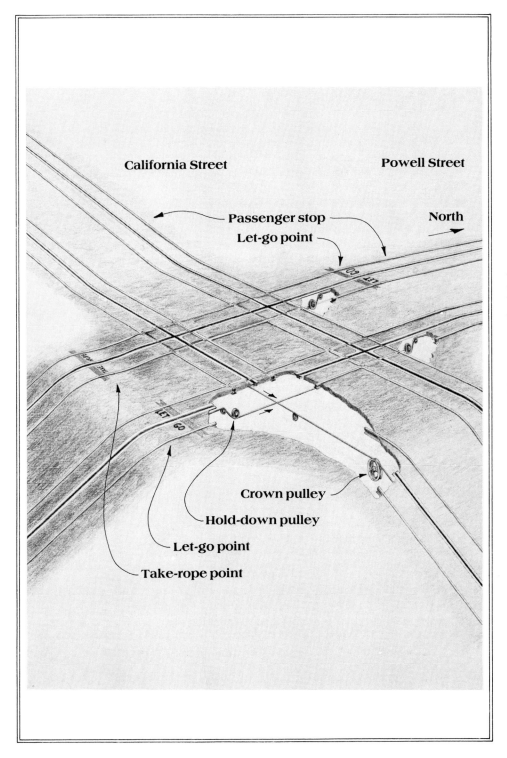

California Street

Powell Street

Passenger stop

Let-go point

North

Crown pulley

Hold-down pulley

Let-go point

Take-rope point

DEPRESSION PULLEYS

The depression pulley is an ingenious device designed to allow passage of the grip and yet restrain the rope from its tendency to take the shortest distance between two points. If the depression pulley were not there, the rope would be wearing against the underside of the slot rails and friction would soon damage it. Always seen at the base of a hill, the depression pulley can be identified by two small, shiny pulleys visible in the slot. These two pulleys are mounted at one end of a tapered bar. The bar is pivoted just beneath the slot and connected to a counterweight at one end. As the grip approaches the depression, the jaws' position below the pulleys forces the rope down and off the pulleys. A moment later the grip shank strikes the narrow end of the bar and since the rope is now off the pulleys the bar is pushed to one side by the forward movement of the grip. When the grip is clear the counterweight forces the bar to swing back into position. The pulleys are then in line with the rope. As soon as the grip is a few feet beyond the depression the rope returns to the pulleys. The car's passage through the depression pulley is audible if the passenger is ready for it. A couple of sharp clicks are heard as the bar is struck and when it swings back into position.

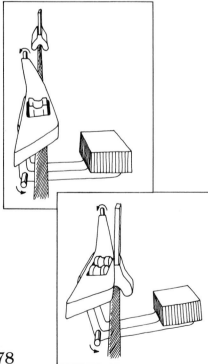

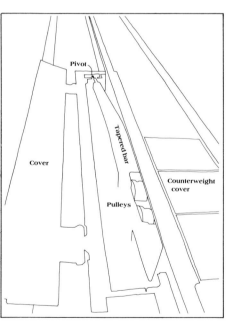

MAINTENANCE

Maintaining the cable car system is virtually a constant effort. Tired machinery, heavy wear and antiquated practices all contribute to the work load. Within the car barn at Mason and Washington streets are areas for each task. On the first floor — maintenance of winding machinery, the rope and an area for rebuilding grips; above and in the car storage area — painting, body work, trucks and cleaning fill the workday. Out on the lines there is always at least one man, the oiler, walking the tracks. Each pulley must be frequently oiled and checked, so the oiler walks down the streets, dodging automobiles, and lifts up each cover plate to apply oil. Occasionally major work must be done, such as replacing the winding sheaves (1965); rebuilding the curves on Columbus Avenue (1970); cleaning and rebuilding the turntables at Bay and Taylor and within the yards (1970).

Splicing a break or replacing a tired rope is one of the more interesting operations, but unfortunately it usually is done sometime between 1:00 a.m. and 6:00 a.m. If a rope breaks, which is rare, a temporary splice must be done just to get it moving again so a permanent splice can be made in the barn. The first warning of an impending break can come in two ways. Hopefully a strand alarm, of which there are several, is struck by the first broken strand. The machinery is then shut down and the loose strand is replaced unless it is apparent that the rope is beginning to break, in which case a complete splice is done. The second warning is what the strand alarms are there to prevent, for if they don't contact the first broken strand it will strike, sooner or later, the back of a grip. Since the crotch is just wide enough for the normal rope diameter, the strand gets caught and cannot pass through. This causes the other strands (there are six main strands of 19 wires each) to break and unravel in rapid succession, piling up like spaghetti within and behind the grip. Meanwhile the cable car is helpless to stop and continues until it meets an obstruction — another cable car, automobiles or anything else in its path.

Once the break has occurred it must be located and a temporary splice done. The machinery is then re-started and the splice is pulled into the barn, where a permanent splice (about 60 feet long and no greater than the normal diameter of the rope) is made. During this process all service is suspended, as the temporary splice is not strong enough to carry the car's weight.

Eventually each tension sheave reaches a certain point signaling the maximum stretching its rope can take. New rope is then threaded

In the dark vaults beneath the corner of Washington and Mason streets. Four ropes are visible as dark blurred lines moving from left to right. At center left is a small two-pronged fork around one rope. This fork, part of a strand alarm, is connected to a warning bell which sounds if a loose strand strikes the fork.

Changing grips in the yards with the aid of a small crane. One shopman is inside the car about to guide the rebuilt grip into the hole. The worn-out grip sits at left.

through the system. After the lines are shut down around 1:00 a.m. the operation is begun by placing the new reel to one side of the tension racks with a take-up spool on the other side. The old rope is cut and the new one is temporarily spliced to it. The sheaves are started, pulling the new rope off its spool and into the streets as the old is taken up on the other spool. In time a complete circuit is made and the temporary splice returns to the barn, where a permanent splice is made to join both ends into a new loop. Finally the rope is lubricated with a coating of tar, leaving it prepared for service.

A slightly more visible operation is the rebuilding of grips. Among the lathes and grinders on the first floor is one little area with grips standing like patients in a waiting room. One man is constantly rebuilding grips, keeping them in circulation as the dies wear out.

Occasionally the rider will notice a gripman tightening the grip adjustment rod, without success, as the car continues to slip back on hills. Usually this means the dies are completely worn out and are losing grip. If the gripman can, he proceeds to the tracks near the barn, but if that's not possible a new grip is brought to him by tow truck. Whatever the case, the gripman positions the car over two small doors in the slot which allow the outsize crotch to pass up and out. The operation begins by opening the car's front doors and disconnecting the grip from the truck by removing two pins locking it on the carry bars. Next the worn grip is lifted out by block and tackle and the new one is lifted in — all by muscle. Then the pins are replaced, doors closed, and the rope regained — movement begins again.

At any given time visitors can see many different operations taking place in and around the storage area on the second floor of the car barn. Probably the most common ones are replacing of the wooden track brake blocks or steel brake shoes and generally checking and adjusting various brakes, levers and other underbody mechanisms. Lubrication is also a frequent task, as there are no closed lubrication systems as on automobiles; everything is greased or oiled as it appears to need it rather than every 12,000 miles — and some of these machines have gone a great deal more than 12,000 miles.

During daytime working hours there is usually at least one car in either the painting or carpentry area. Automobiles intruding on the cable car's right of way at the wrong moment almost succeed in keeping wooden coachbuilding alive. Each accident usually ruins one automobile and causes only minor damage to the cable car, but occasionally one really gets it and that means days of careful woodworking. Painting follows, for otherwise dry rot would set in, as the majority of the cable car is wood. Wear from countless tourists' feet and shoulders rubbing on door frames in combination with time eventually catches up with the paint. As a result some of the cars have almost developed a separate structure composed of layers of paint.

Car 504 in the process of having its rear platform rebuilt after being rammed by another cable car. The hardwood framing of the roof is clearly visible.

Some of the car barn tracks have pits which allow the underside mechanism to be easily reached. Here car 507 is resting over one such pit with its protruding grip barely visible silhouetted in the center of the photograph.

SCENE ONE

A young gripman working car 514 — waiting for clearance at the Bay and Taylor turntable. His leather gloves riding the brake handle as if attached — he seems to glance, with no movement of head, at those passing on the car which just left the table. It's clear now — right hand moves to grasp the grip's polished end. He's standing sideways — no body movement to pull the grip — only the curling action of a strong forearm — cool, very cool. This one brisk movement and the car rolls forward — he's now in a position of alert stare ready to release. Rolling till past the "let go" point — 'course he knows where it is without looking — no, still not a glance forward. Then, at the last moment he snaps right, knowing time of action. Hand pulls back from its rest in space — two inches and the grip's ratchet is released with a crack. By now he's turned to face the front — stopping on the table must be precise as there isn't much extra track — the left hand has smoothly found the brake handle. His entire body moves with the grip lever all the way forward to full release — a moment of ballet from someone whose previous demeanor suggested Marine Corps. Rope now out of jaws as the car rolls around a slight turn. Hollow rumble — steel wheels on rails, wooden deck and concrete pit — a clicking ratchet as he applies the brake, no more rumble. No movement either, except our gripman dismounting with peripheral glances — casual, though still cool. Don't know if anyone else saw — maybe he knows. Turning the car he's intense as this task requires so much physical strength there is no space for distractions. After the car is turned a handful of passengers notice him standing as the land ship captain eyes staring blankly — waiting for act three. Gypsy up, rope regained — conductor jumps on and our man pulls the grip back — moves the car forward, still slipping. A second and stronger movement makes the car surge — up to nine point five miles per hour. He disappears behind the other cars — awaiting a turnaround.

SCENE TWO

The storage barn above Mason Street — cable cars are kept for the
night. A yard allows them movement in and out — of their stalls and daily
rounds. Late evening hours — each car would roll in from its daily
run — gravity carrying them into their repair and morning arena. An arena
lit by a few overhead lamps and populated by men's machinery —
Mechanics inhabit a corrugated steel shack at one end of the yard.
I'd walk in — immersed immediately in oily steel smells — a kind,
soft-spoken man whom I had met before was working the night shift. We
talked — for he challenged me in a subtle way — experience had given him
rooms I hadn't entered for he was much older than myself. On my
previous walks into his night realm we had talked mainly of cable
cars — nuts and bolts — tonight city politics was covered to our own
distinct limits. Out on Jackson a car would rumble through the
switch — noise sometimes followed by sudden silence — clanging of a
single bell — audible insistence. My friend breaks conversation — a brief
task must be done — he walks briskly to the switch. A car waits to enter
the yard — gripman and conductor alone — prepared to release brakes as
soon as the switch is open. Sound was my only information — heard the
switch click followed by the brakes release — then rumbling of steel
rolling over joints, increasing as the car rounded the turn — decreasing
closer, closer, slower approaching turntable. Now in my view — suddenly
illuminated by an overhead lamp — car onto table — brakes then applied
with a slight screech. Some words — "grip needs replacement, put on
track three" — my friend helps turn the car as the gripman and conductor
pass me — going to the locker room and probably some coffee — a smoke.
I catch the sound of the car rolling into track three — the hollow sound of
the wooden floor absorbing the weight — six tons pushing boards
down — stressing nails till they yell. Friend returns — conversation fades
soon — lost thread. I walked on toward Broadway — the warmth of our
brief conversation clothing my mind as I moved among cold chrome
midnight people.

SCENE THREE

     Large diesel truck carrying unpainted cable car through San Francisco streets. Backing into Jackson Street yard entrance. Cable car number 523, groaning as trailer twists over incoming track — stretching tie-down chains. Now the crowd assembles — mechanics, aficionados — greasy hands — hands on camera shutters. The operation begins — while truckdriver prepares to winch the car off the trailer — group of mechanics construct temporary wooden ramp. Two by fours, by sixes, by twelves on top of one another — steel channels to function as rails. Result — loose little piers of odds and ends — a bridge from trailer to rails. Substantial? no — didn't cost a penny though. The first movement — barely a crawl — some squeaking as steel shears steel — thump! — onto ramp. Winch barely moving as chain vibrates from tension — car continues down ramp. Concentration is broken — a loud grating snap — all eyes move to nail holding end of ramp to ground. Quick — pull the car back up. Car would have fallen over had it continued down. Intense men — one with hammer driving nails back into asphalt, another repositioning the wooden piers — should hold now. Winch into gear again — thump! — onto the ramp — no snap now, it must be tight — it held until the front wheels dropped off — then another snap — wasn't serious now as the car was almost off the ramp. It ended up with the front wheels on the pavement. Some small wedges and a tow car pulling — bumps back onto steel — the final, solid thud as shock of steel striking steel follows a wooden frame — sound deadened as it progresses. The new 523 is moved back into yard — number known only by chalk marks on primed steel. Its gray contorted Bombay roof was from another car — the tiny windows still open — guess it was thought a shame to let the roof go to waste just because the body beneath it was rotten.

     Catching attention from assembled crowd — car number 502 pulled out into the sun — its rear platform crushed and folded — rammed by another car — a final blow, she couldn't take any more. Her joints revealed rotting wood beneath the curling paint — from a distance a bent frame was obvious. Time's up — then 502 is up and onto the trailer — the group not interested now — nothing new. Tie-down chains fastened and tightened. The few men left take up the little ramp — truckdriver turns over the diesel — from silence to roar — gears mesh — but only with complaints. Audience scatters — back in to work — must keep hands greased — truck can be heard — roar of exhaust up Jackson Street — shifts at Taylor — wrench dropped nearby — back to normal.

as it
was

The Baldwin Hotel, built by "Lucky"
Baldwin, who struck it rich in the California
gold fields. This photograph was taken in the
1860's across Market from its intersection
with Powell. Four horsecar tracks are visible
down Market at right, while two cross
Market and proceed up Powell. The broad
white lines crossing the streets were granite
panels set within the cobblestones to mark a
crosswalk. Four black cabs are visible parked
on Market Street. The building was destroy-
ed in the earthquake and fire of 1906.

San Francisco is a reluctant city. Her hills are steep, her bay is hidden; she had a propensity at the outset to burn to the ground at regular intervals, and she remains notorious for shaking buildings from their foundations. She eluded centuries of explorers who sailed unknowingly past her valuable harbor — Cortes, Drake, Cabrillo, Ulloa, Cermento, Vizcaino — until the overland expedition of Portola and Father Serra finally viewed her in 1769. And even then she stayed relatively uncivilized as the sleepy Spanish hamlet of Yerba Buena until the Gold Rush of 1849 transformed her overnight into the city of San Francisco and swelled her population of 812 souls to 25,000 residents. In the madness of urbanization that followed, her citizens — through no small effort — succeeded in domesticating her. And the cable car was, among other things, an instrument of that domestication.

But the cable car was not the city's first attempt at public transportation; in fact, it did not make its appearance on San Francisco streets till the 1870's. The initial effort in the interest of public transportation in San Francisco was made in 1850, while the city was still seized by gold frenzy, prices were skyrocketing, and vigilantism prevailed. An eight-year franchise was granted for the construction of a plank-paved toll road on Folsom and Mission streets. Construction was expensive and tolls ranged from 25 cents for a horse and rider to one dollar for a four-horse team. By 1852 the first public conveyance — the "Yellow Line" omnibus service — was running between the Post Office, at Clay and Kearny streets, and Mission Dolores, for the whopping fares of 50 cents on weekdays and one dollar on Sundays. A second route was added in 1854, a third in 1855 and by 1857 several more routes were in operation, with the fares uniformly reduced to 10 cents.

A horsecar on Market at Kearny Street evidently paused while the cameraman made his long exposure. It seems no one was able to convince the horses to stand still.

In 1860 steam cars were introduced in San Francisco, but these cumbersome vehicles, although more powerful, were not as popular as the horse cars, which continued to dominate the transportation system. Langley's City Directory offered this explanation:

> It is hardly too much to say that the modern horse car is among the most indispensable conditions of modern metropolitan growth. It is to a city what steam car and steamship lines are to the state and country. In these days of fashionable effeminacy and flabby feebleness, one never walks when one can possibly ride. The horse car virtually frees the ultimate limits of suburban growth.

San Francisco was still growing, however, and cultivating a sophistication that the "hay burners" could not accommodate, Langley's exuberance notwithstanding. Accidents were frequent, the horses were inhumanely overworked — the average life of a railway horse was only 4½ years — and the city's steep hills remained an unsolved transportation problem. One early critic had an interesting observation in this regard: "If the City had been laid out with respect to its topography, the hillsides terraced...(it) would have been more picturesque...As it is, poetry and beauty have succumbed to the practical and ugly." If the hillsides had in fact been terraced in the beginning, it is likely that neither the need for nor the invention of San Francisco's cable cars would have occurred. Fortunately or not, San Franciscans seemingly preferred the direct route up the imposing rises, and the horse and steam cars were inadequate.

Thus, the appearance of the steamless, hayless, almost noiseless, thankfully non-excremental, ably hill-climbing cable car in 1873 was a heralded event. Applause came from the SPCA and the Mechanics' Institute alike, and the hero of the hour — once the cable car had proved itself in an official demonstration — was Andrew Smith Hallidie.

Hallidie was born in London in 1836. His father, a Scotsman, was an engineer and inventor who held wire rope patents dating from 1835 to 1849. Hallidie's early training was, therefore, both scientific and mechanical. At 13 he began working in his brother's machine shop and drafting office, and by all accounts even as a child was unusually industrious and inventive.

In 1852, at the age of 16, Hallidie accompanied his father to California to investigate an interest in the Fremont Estate, and it was here in California that Andrew Hallidie was to make his home. Predictably, soon after landing he was off to the mining fields with the droves of fortune seekers who had migrated to California from all parts of the globe. Hallidie's success with the pick and pan was negligible, but his skills in blacksmithy, surveying, and building proved profitable in the California gold country, and these years provided the experience that was to establish him professionally in San Francisco.

In 1855, when he was just 19, Andrew Hallidie accomplished the construction of a wire suspension viaduct over 200 feet long across the middle fork of the American River. In 1856 he began to manufacture metal rope, using one of his father's inventions, and in the years that followed took out many patents for his own inventions. Among these was the "Hallidie Ropeway or Tramway," which matured in 1867-69 — a system for transporting ore and other materials in the mines by means of an overhead endless traveling cable. By the end of the 1860's, Hallidie had established himself in San Francisco as A.S. Hallidie and Company, making wire cables in an unpretentious building at Mason and Chestnut streets. Recalling 1869, the inventor later wrote:

> My attention was called to the great difficulty experienced in hauling the street cars...up one of the steep streets of the City of San Francisco, and the great cruelty and hardship to the horses engaged in that work. With the view of obviating these difficulties, and for the purpose of reducing the expense of operating street railways...I devoted all my available time to the careful consideration of the subject.

However, the idea for a cable railway, or in fact even the application of that idea to city transportation, did not originate with Hallidie, though the ingenuity with which he applied the principle to San Francisco's steep hills has been quite justly commended. In other parts of the United States and abroad, cable street railways were proposed as early as 1812. A patent request was made by Messrs. W. and E. Chapman in that year; a similar request in 1824 by W. James; M. Dick in 1829; W.J. Curtis in

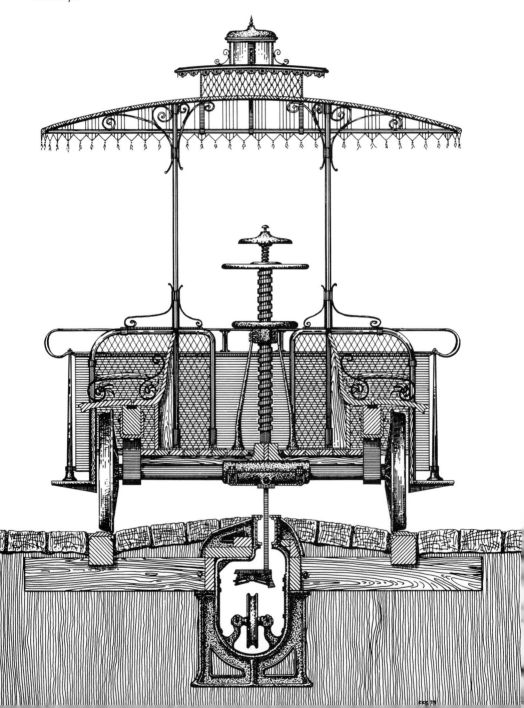

Cross-section of a very early cable car showing Hallidie's original grip design, which involved a screwing action rather than a lever. This method was later found to be too slow in gaining a grip on the cable. Note the wooden rails covered with iron straps.

1845; and in 1858 by E.S. Gardiner in Philadelphia, whose particular scheme has been credited with establishing the principles by which all subsequent ones were devised. Among others who registered patent applications were W. Greaves in 1860, P. W. Barlow in 1864, A. Thompson and J. Roberts in 1872. And apparently even in San Francisco there was at least one other person besides Hallidie who entertained notions of cable transportation before the fact. A man by the name of Benjamin Brooks held a franchise for an undefined cable haulage scheme in the city, and it has been suggested that it was from Brooks that Hallidie acquired the franchise under which he finally operated.

While Hallidie was developing San Francisco's first cable car system, cable transportation devices similar to the sort Hallidie had employed in the California mines were being used extensively in other parts of the world—in sugar cane transporting in Brazil and Peru, and in the salt mines of the Indian government in Punjab; for fireclay transporting in Bohemia, and by the Spanish government's mining industry in the Asturian mountains. Nonetheless, application of the principle to the transportation of people was still an unproved proposition, and when it came to finding money to finance his venture, Hallidie met with considerable skepticism. San Franciscans, blessed or cursed as they were with the Gold Rush gains in the '50's and the fortunes of the Nevada Comstock Lode in the '60's, were by the '70's up to their ears in speculation and considerably less eager to invest in something they had no guarantee would bring a return. Hallidie succeeded only in enlisting the support of three old friends, Joseph Britton, Henry L. Davis and James Moffit—all of whom had a common interest in the building of the Mechanics' Institute. With their backing, a company was finally organized in 1872.

Hallidie had originally intended to try his cable schemes on the California Street hill and in 1870 had it surveyed for the purpose by an engineer named David R. Smith. Smith, however, left shortly afterward for a job in South America and Hallidie was forced to abandon the plan temporarily. With the forming of his company in 1872, Hallidie substituted Clay Street for California in his plans because there were more houses and construction costs would be lower; thus a new survey was made, and stock was offered to the public.

For the most part, however, the stock remained available, for only $28,000 was collected from private investors. Hallidie himself was forced to contribute $20,000 to the project, his three friends gave about $40,000, and an additional $30,000 had to be secured on a 10-year loan through the Clay Street Bank at 10 percent interest.

The trial run of Hallidie's car came on August 2, 1873, just in time to meet the franchise deadline, at an hour early enough to avoid a gathering of doubting onlookers. The small party that met to witness the crucial test consisted of Hallidie and his three partners; his draftsman,

William Eppelsheimer; Assistant Superintendent P. H. Campbell; the bookkeeper, Thomas P. Burns; and the now-famous reluctant gripman. It may or may not be fact that the terrified would-be gripman shrank from his post murmuring something about his wife and children — or as a 19th-century writer put it, he "succumbed to cogent skepticism regarding the reliability of the scheme and his personal safety." But it is a matter of record that Hallidie himself at last manned the grip on the historic run and was sufficiently satisfied with its success to schedule an official demonstration that afternoon.

Mayor William Alvord, Chief of Police Patric Crowley, Fire Chief David Scannell, Sheriff James Adams and other prominent city officials and businessmen were present at the official run, in addition to the crowd who had turned out "to see if the damned thing worked." After a mishap with a broken belt connecting the grip with the car frame, causing a delay of 20 minutes or so, the official run began. It turned out to be a greater test than Hallidie had planned: enthusiasm to take part in the first public demonstration was quite literally overwhelming and people climbed on wherever they could — some hanging on to the guard rail, others actually on the roof. Ninety bodies aboard a car designed for 30! The cable car nonetheless performed successfully and the event marked a new era in San Francisco's public transportation.

An early cable car of the Clay Street Hill Railroad preparing to depart up Clay from Kearny, probably around 1874. Portsmouth Square is to the left. At this point the cable car was still a simple demonstration without the complications of a full-fledged transport system.

On the windy heights of Nob Hill at Clay and Mason streets around 1875. The construction of the cable car system allowed these sparsely developed hilltops to become blocks of Victorian homes, later giving way to apartment buildings and hotels.

Everyone frozen for the camera's long exposure. On the Clay street line at Jones just before descending downtown around 1875. Note the elaborate striping on the trailer.

The Clay Street Hill Company began regular operations in September of 1873, and its popularity was evidenced by substantial earnings from the start. That year Hallidie's company recorded an average monthly net earning of $3,000, profits from the modest five-cent fares at which reluctant investors had scoffed.

Andrew Hallidie became a wealthy and respected citizen of San Francisco as a result of his inventiveness and aptitude for commercial venture, together with his apparently genuine civic interest. He participated actively in the establishment of the Mechanics' Institute, the California School of Mechanical Arts and the Wilmerding Training School. Hallidie also was instrumental in the framing of the San Francisco charter and served as a regent of the University of California from its inception in 1868 until his death in 1900. Until the structure was remodeled in the 1940's, a plaque on the Hallidie Building on Sutter Street paid public homage to Hallidie:

HALLIDIE BUILDING
NAMED IN HONOR OF
ANDREW SMITH HALLIDIE
BORN IN LONDON ENGLAND
MARCH SIXTEEN 1836
DIED IN SAN FRANCISCO
APRIL TWENTY-FOUR 1900 —
CREATOR OF OUR CABLE RAILWAY — TWICE
MEMBER OF A BOARD OF FREEHOLDERS
CHOSEN TO FRAME A CHARTER
FOR THIS CITY — REGENT OF THE
UNIVERSITY FROM THE FIRST MEETING
OF THE BOARD JUNE NINE 1868 TO
THE DAY OF HIS DEATH — DURING HIS
LAST TWENTY-SIX YEARS DEVOTED
CHAIRMAN OF ITS FINANCE COMMITTEE
BUILDER CITIZEN REGENT
A MAN OF INTEGRITY

The success of Hallidie's cable line created a surge of new interest in San Francisco transportation. Men who had paid little attention to "Hallidie's Folly" while it was still on the drawing board and in need of funds to begin operation now saw an opportunity for profit, and a rush was on for the city's street railway franchises. Notable among the newcomers was Leland Stanford, former governor of California and a member of the Central Pacific Railroad's "Big Four." His plan was to install a system similar to Hallidie's on California Street that would furnish the wealthy residents of Nob Hill, or "Snob Hill" as some called it, with sorely needed transportation. Suprisingly, in spite of Hallidie's success, even the influential Stanford had some trouble interesting backers in the projected California Street line. Mark Hopkins, another member of the "Big Four," said with classic irony, "It is as likely to pay a dividend as the 'Hotel de Hopkins' " —a reference to his private residence

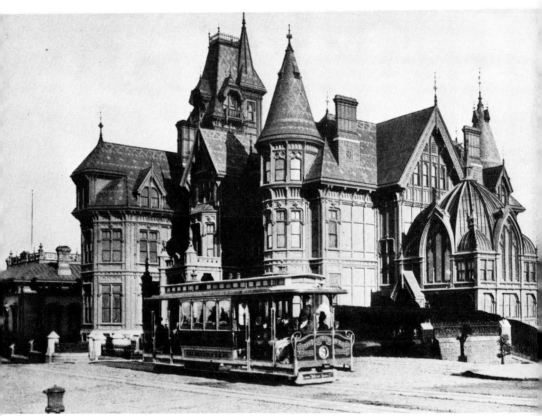

At California and Mason looking southeast towards the present
site of the Mark Hopkins Hotel. The meager residence was, as
the postcard caption specifies, the home of Mr. Hopkins. Mr.
Stanford was apparently satisfied with the slums around Powell
and California. This picture shows what was meant by the use
of the term "Snob Hill." The California car in the foreground
is similar to existing cars in general layout only. All the California
cars of this type were destroyed by fire in 1906.

then under construction, which is now the site of the prestigious Mark Hopkins Hotel. Like Hallidie, Stanford eventually was forced to purchase much of his company's stock himself—reportedly 4,700 of 5,000 shares—and some observers said that he privately resigned himself to indulging in the cable endeavor as a hobby. His intention, in any case, was to build the finest cable line possible, and that is precisely what he did.

Stanford hired Henry Root, a well known and respected engineer from Vermont, whom he instructed to "study up" on the system and to assemble the best qualified staff he could find. With the indisputable advantages of time, talent and resources, Root oversaw the building of San Francisco's most advanced cable car line to date, characterized by mechanical innovation, safety, luxury and convenience. By his own admission, Root in fact had been defensive about infringing on certain of Hallidie's patent rights early in the building of Stanford's line.

Of course, Hallidie himself was concerned with protecting patent rights—with good reason. He controlled broad patents relating to almost all facets of cable traction and was justly anxious to collect a profit on the use of his patent methods whenever possible. Hallidie's Clay Street Company therefore advanced an offer of consultation and assistance to the California Street Company, for a monetary compensation in the neighborhood of $40,000. Further, Hallidie's company offered to subscribe for one half of the capitol stock if the construction plans met with their approval. Stanford's reply was prompt, indignant and succinct: "If I undertake to build the California Street road I am going to be the one to determine what plans will be used and if our lawyers say that we are infringing on patents we will pay, if we must, for the privilege of using them." From then on communication between the two companies was purely of a legal nature, reflecting the rivalry that cable transportation had inherited from the horse car lines. Eventually Stanford's company was legally forced to pay Hallidie $30,000 for a license to operate under his patent rights.

Patent entanglements did not deter the public opening of the California Street Line in April of 1878, however. Like the champagne opening of the Sutter Street line by street railway innovator Henry Casebolt the year before, it was a gala affair. The event drew a crowd of over 6,000 persons, city officials lent dignity to the occasion and many major businesses closed for the festivities. Both Nob Hill and Western Addition residents were likewise jubilant; the new line furnished them with excellent public transportation, and property values quickly reflected the improvement.

In general, real estate gains were increased sizably wherever cable lines were extended, usually to triple the value in formerly inaccessible areas. With few exceptions, new lines proved commercially profitable for everyone concerned—owners, investors, riders, property owners and merchants alike.

This photograph was taken in the 1890's looking west from Presidio Avenue out California Street. In the distance can be seen the smoke and vague image of a steam locomotive which was probably pulling a train bound for Land's End and the Cliff House. An empty California car stands waiting for passengers while another waits at end of track.

In 1882 just west of Union Square on the Geary Street line a gripcar with its open trailer was caught on film. The bystander in the background apparently stayed for only part of the exposure. Open cars were common on many cable lines and relied on canvas flaps in event of rain.

On the Polk Street line of the Sutter Street railroad out on Pacific Avenue near the end of the line at Broderick Street. This was probably taken early in the morning, which would account for the lack of pedestrians or passengers.

The success of cable car systems is evidenced by the proliferation of new lines in the years that followed Hallidie's 1873 achievement. Stanford's California Street line and Casebolt's line on Sutter Street started the trend, although Casebolt's attempt may have been ill-advised. It was plagued by "eternal repairs and patching," and one irate citizen recommended that "tracks, roadbed, cars and all should be sold to the junk man." The Geary Street, Park & Ocean Railroad and the Presidio & Ferries Railroad both began operation in 1880; the Market Street Railway, employing the city's choicest franchises, in 1883; the Ferries and Cliff House Railroad, which acquired the original Clay Street Hill Railroad, in 1888; and the Omnibus Cable Company in 1888, a converted horse car line dating back to 1863, which as a cable line eventually proved an unsuccessful competitor to the Market Street company. In 1884, a man named Layman tried a counterbalance system on Telegraph Hill, similar to the system experimented with on Fillmore Street—a descending car which lifted an ascending one by the force of its weight. It failed financially, however, and was dubbed "Layman's Folly."

At the height of cable transportation in the city during the 1880's and early 1890's, tracks stretched a total of 112 miles—112 miles of cut-throat competition, patent battles, profit-making and riders who were gradually developing a tremendous affection for the cable car. Among them was Rudyard Kipling, who wrote in 1889:

> They take no count of rise or fall, but slide equably on their appointed courses from one end to the other of a six-mile street. They turn corners almost at right angles; cross other lines and for all I know may run up the side of houses. There is no visible agency for their flight; but once in a while you shall pass a five storied building humming with machinery that winds up an everlasting wire cable and the initiated will tell you that here is the mechanism. I gave up asking questions. If it pleases Providence to make a car run up and down a slit in the ground for many miles and if for two pence-half penny I can ride in that car, why shall I seek the reason of the miracle?

Seeds of sentimentalism and local pride were sown by such offerings as "The Ballad of the Hyde Street Grip," by Gelett Burgess, which included the following lines:

> If you had to drive a penny bus from Chelsea to the Strand
> You'd see Westminister Abbey, and you'd say that it was grand!
> If you had to pass the Luxembourg and Place de la Concorde
> Atop a Paris omnibus, no doubt you'd thank the Lord!
> But the Frenchy'd give his chapeau and the Cockney'd give his whip
> For the sight of San Francisco from the Hyde Street Grip!

Cable cars permeated San Francisco life. Besides revolutionizing crosstown transportation, they had a great impact on the recreation habits of San Franciscans. Conveniently accessible by cable car were such places as the Presidio, Castle amusement center atop Telegraph Hill, Golden Gate Park, Woodward's Gardens—an amusement park on Mission Street—and the well-kept cemetaries where, oddly enough, a good deal of socializing went on in those days. The cable car managements had a vested interest in organized weekend entertainment, which met with enthusiastic patronage by the thrill-seeking San Franciscans—such events as "Professor" Baldwin's famous balloon ascension and parachute drops at Baker's Beach and the daring Millie Lavelle, who slid on a wire rope stretched from the Cliff House to the beach, hanging—how else?—by her teeth.

Cable cars were not the exclusive property of San Franciscans at this point in their history, however. Hallidie's success and the prosperity of those who followed him in San Francisco became well known both here and abroad. For several decades at the height of their popularity, cable cars were in use in many U.S. cities, including Seattle, Los Angeles, New York, Philadelphia, Chicago, Cleveland, St. Louis, Kansas City, Denver and Oakland, as well as cities in New Zealand, Australia, England and the Continent. In 1890 there were an estimated 500 miles of cable track in the United States upon which some 5,000 cars carried an average of 4,000,000 passengers per year.

On Market looking due west, with Haight Street leading to the right. At near left a bluff is visible, just above an inbound cable car. The United States Mint stands there today. Notice the bare outline of twin peaks to the left. This photograph was probably taken around 1900, when outer Market Street was sparsely developed. The two tripod-like objects standing in the center were probably set up to lift something very heavy off a wagon.

*Looking up Greenwich Street on the short-lived Telegraph Hill Railroad
(1884-1886). This line served the Castle Amusement Center of the top
of Telegraph Hill at upper right and was known as ''Layman's Folly.'' In
this scene one car is moving into the passing track, while another is on
its way up. The passing track was halfway up and obviated the need for
double track over the whole five-block route.*

The peak of cable operations in San Francisco was reached in the early 1890's, followed by a period of consolidation and a gradual decline influenced largely by the advent of the electric trolley car. The principal cable railways of the city were consolidated in 1893, and United Railroads of San Francisco took over operation of the Market Street, Sutter, Sutro and San Mateo lines in 1902, by which time the nation's 500 miles of cable track had been reduced by half.

But the year 1906 delivered a far more devastating blow to San Francisco's cable system than all the combined conditions of its decline. At that time, San Francisco was again enjoying one of its many periods of prosperity. Money came easily, prices were up, soundly financed corporations were yielding satisfactory returns. The population trend continued favorable, and extensive construction was going on in the Western Addition to accommodate the increase. Automobiles—innocent oddities then—had just begun to appear on the city's streets and though electric trolleys were faster, cable transportation was still popular and a fairly good stock to be holding.

The earthquake and fire of April 18, 1906, brought it all to a standstill. Just when the morning cars were circulating on their first runs the shock struck, at 5:13 a.m. Three days later the city was in ruins—the financial, wholesale, retail and shopping districts had been leveled. Over 28,000 buildings were destroyed, and property loss was estimated as high as $400,000,000. Cable car tracks were twisted and pulled away from the streets in a confusion of debris and crumpled pavement. A description of the California Street Company's engine house, from J.B. Stetson's Personal Recollections During the Eventful Days of April, 1906, typifies the scene:

> Beams, pipes, iron columns, tie-rods, car-trucks, and a tangled mess of ironwork, bricks, mortar, ashes, and debris of every description filled the place. The interior was unbearably hot...Seemingly everything was there, but rods, cranks, beams and pipes were out of shape and badly damaged...The prospect of ever repairing and getting the machinery and appliances in operation again seemed impossible.

The initial shock of the quake paralyzed the massive drums in the cable engine houses; steam connections to boilers were broken, engines loosened on their bed plates, and damage to slots and rails was extensive enough to end the career of many of the remaining cable car lines. The holocaust that followed consumed what was left of three of the system's powerhouses and at least one-fourth of the city's 400 cable cars.

Many of the Market Street cable cars that had escaped damage were later converted to temporary dwellings for some of the 300,000 homeless refugees of the disaster. Cars operating west of Van Ness Avenue when the earthquake struck were in large part saved, but the central transportation system in the heart of the ruined city was destroyed.

This photograph, which the Rainier Beer company will surely appreciate, was probably taken from the Ferry Building tower. Market Street diminishes in the thick smog which was normal on still days when coal and oil were common fuels. At the bottom the four tracks of the Market Street Cable Railway Company branch out to accommodate all the cars waiting for passengers from the many ferryboats. It was probably taken around 1900 Just to the right of center can be seen one car on the loop between Sacramento and Clay streets. This is the western terminus of the Clay-Sacramento line of the Ferries and Cliff House Railroad.

Municipal ownership of cable lines began in 1912. The following year, the Board of Supervisors passed a resolution asking an offer from the California Street Company to sell out to the city, but by then the California line had regained its posture as a reasonably lucrative operation and in fact was to remain in private ownership until 1952. On the other hand, such lines as the Presidio and Ferries Railroad Company gradually were taken over by the city when their franchises expired. The years between the earthquake of 1906 and the early 1940's were perhaps the least illustrious in cable car history. They represented, in some respects, a period of decline and obsolescence. By 1940, San Francisco was the only city in North America with a cable system. "Modern" transportation such as electric trolleys, buses and —alas—automobiles now crowded the city's streets. But in another way, this was also a quiet period of gathering sentimentalism. An excerpt from A. Bailey's 1921 Vignettes of San Francisco reflects this benignly affectionate attitude toward the one-time mechanical miracle:

The cable car isn't a car at all, children, but is a hilly-cum-go, a species of rocking horse and a grown-up kiddie-kar. It is a native of and peculiar to San Francisco and is a loyal member of the NSGW. It has relatives in the South, and the electric dinkie that rolls up and down between Venice and Santa Monica is its first cousin. Some say it is related to the wheel chairs at Atlantic City. It is not at all common.

The men who run it are its Uncles. The parents live underground caring for the young kiddie-kars. At times, if you peek down in that hole near the Fairmont and are careful not to be run over, you may see them bustling about. Before she was married, the Mama was Marjory Daw of the Daw family, famous see-sawers. The children take after their mother.

The uncles are very kind and pick the hilly-cum-goes up in their arms as tenderly as a woman would. You must have seen them pick the little things up and run with them across the streets out of the way of autos. And at night they tuck them in their little beds and hear their prayer which goes:

Oh, dear me, I hope I'm able,
All day long to keep my cable.

These hilly-cum-goes are not run by electricity at all, but just pretend. They are run by three things—black magic, white magic, and a sense of humor....

I trust, dear children, that all these facts will make you appreciate more the hilly-cum-go, and when you sit on it so cosy, so intimate with the street, riding along looking at the scenery, you will be thankful that poor old horses do not have to tug you up the hill, and that you have this sturdy little creature to haul you about. Nice little, old hilly-cum-go.

Around noon on April 18th, 1906, looking east on Clay Street just above Stockton. The first shock was the earthquake at 5:13 that morning. Later another form of shock took hold: the realization that San Francisco was burning. The people in this photograph were probably just beginning to feel that shock, as the fire could be observed raging only five blocks away.

California Palace of the Legion of Honor

California Palace of the Legion of Honor

On Union Street looking west from Steiner. This was probably taken on April 18th, only hours after the earthquake struck. In terms of actual damage the earthquake was serious but minor compared to the fire that followed.

Mail car ''A'' operated for a short time carrying sacked mail from outlying postal stations to the mail dock on the waterfront. A mail slot was provided on the side of the car so pedestrians could drop a letter in as the car went by.

San Francisco Public Library

But sentiment was not so warm in the 1940's. Predictably, the cable car was at last faced with real extinction. And a vociferous collection of San Franciscans and tourists from around the world rose up to prevent it. In 1941, rumor had it that the original Clay Street line was to be replaced by buses. Many citizens indignantly protested what they took to be the scrapping of a San Francisco tradition. Newspapers opposed the plan, and delegations of San Franciscans went before the Board of Supervisors to voice their disapproval. A Save the Cable Car League was formed, but its efforts ultimately failed, and February 15, 1942, saw the final run of the world's first cable car line on Clay Street.

By 1947, when the proposal came to do away with the cable cars altogether, there were precious few remaining. In his annual message to the Board of Supervisors in January of that year, Mayor Roger Lapham — ostensibly in the interest of public convenience and economy — summarily demanded complete removal of what was left of the city's cable railway system. He announced that buses had already been ordered to replace the cable cars and would be delivered "in about thirty days." Lapham had unwittingly committed political suicide.

At first the city reacted with an air of typical sentimentality, lamenting the end of an era with passive acceptance. The local papers ran stories with such titles as "Doom of Cable Cars Sealed," "The Cable Cars Are on Their Last Legs" and "We'll Miss Them." But a new kind of resentment was stirring and before long the Mayor — the incredibly single-purposed, stern-faced Mayor — had a battle on his hands.

A Powell car in original configuration around 1890. Note ''Bombay'' roof and open front end.

Mayor Lapham's remarkable job of alienating the electorate was highlighted by his ride down Market Street in an old-time horse car — hoping presumably to ridicule the city's reluctance to "progress." His feeling was explicit: the cable car represented an "outmoded, broken-down from of transportation....The horse cars had to go, and the cable cars have to go." But his performance on Market Street merely restated the case against him. He had inadvertently illustrated the charm of the extinct horse car and prompted many San Franciscans to suggest that it might even be a good idea to bring a few of them back along with the cable cars. Lapham also continued to stir the debate with such sarcasms as "San Franciscans who like bumping the bumps and riding the curves (should) find their enjoyment in the chutes, scenic railway or spinno-rocket at the beach."

Prominent in the campaign to save the cable cars was Mrs. Hans Klussman, wife of a San Francisco surgeon and central figure in the San Francisco Federation of Arts. She headed the new and widely publicized Citizens' Committee to Save the Cable Cars, a committee so effective that it seemed far more than a group of loosely organized amateurs. In fact, Mrs. Klussman was asked more than once if she had employed the services of some national agency. No need: San Franciscans were on the warpath, with no intention of being bullied by an elected official who in their estimation was ignoring their expressed wishes. Mrs. Klussman spoke for them: "To me, stopping the cable cars would (be) like ripping the heart out of the City."

An open car on Market Street. Passengers probably enjoyed these cars in warm weather but cable companies found them a liability when the balance sheet leaned to red.

The Mayor was surrounded, outnumbered, overwhelmed. San Francisco teemed with cable car supporters—national celebrities, private citizens, little children, civic groups and service organizations. Cable car poems were written and recited, a concert orchestra played Glen Hurlburt's "Cable Car Concerto," a cable car art show was held at the City of Paris and cable car songs were sung in night clubs and music halls. Letters-to-the-editor in defense of the cable system deluged the city's papers, many protesting bitterly at being crowded into the "lurching, stifling buses." Polls were conducted which confirmed again and again the cable car's popularity. Stores such as Macy's and the Emporium capitalized on the mood with a stock of dresses in cable car prints. National coverage of the controversy was extensive: Time, Life, Saturday Evening Post and all of the wire services carried articles about the citizens' campaign to save the cable cars.

The Mayor's supporters were few and succeeded in becoming villains in the public eye with him; among them were the ciy's Public Utilities Commission, the San Francisco Real Estate Board, and of course the bus manufacturers and their salesmen. Curiously, cable historian E.M. Kahn apparently was also in this camp. At various public meetings he was heard to say, "I'm no sentimental fool, I want buses on California Street and as soon as possible." It was later observed by one cable car aficionado that sales of Kahn's popular cable car book, then in its ninth printing, "declined appropriately."

A rather austere car of the Market Street Railway Company at the Castro and 26th streets turntable around 1940. Buses took over this route on April 5, 1941.

May 15th, 1954: the last run on the O'Farrell-Jones Street lines, once part of the California Street Cable Railroad, which had been incorporated into the Municipal Railway in 1952. These two lines started at Jones and Market and O'Farrell-Market. From those intersections the tracks went up to the intersection of Jones and O'Farrell. Then as one line the tracks were laid north up Jones to Pine turning west to Hyde then north to California Street. The sign at upper left reads "What sort of city government is this?" "The people want cable cars 13 to 1." "To work so hard against the wishes of the people!"

The citizens were sentimental, maybe, but they were not fools. The sustained efforts of the overwhelming majority of San Francisco's population, in words, actions and finally in votes, succeeded in saving the cable cars — the few that remained by the end of the seven-year battle — from the hands of the pragmatists. In 1955 the San Francisco city charter incorporated an article guaranteeing the perpetuation of the three remaining lines, California, Powell-Mason and Powell-Hyde, a mandate which cannot be amended or revoked without the approval of a majority of San Francisco voters — an unlikely eventuality.

Cable cars, albeit in token numbers, continue to run on San Francisco streets and serve in private ownership — the city has sold about 30 since World War II for bids as high as $3,000 — as snack bars, bath houses, greenhouses, duck blinds and gazebos. Motorized cars, also privately owned, are rented to companies for promotional purposes and to conventions for touring and trips between hotels. As an unmistakable symbol of the city, the cars are loaned for use in movie-making, television and special exhibitions and perhaps promote more tourism in San Francisco than any one other city attraction.

Cable car sentiment was formalized in February of 1964. A plaque was fixed to the wall of the one remaining cable engine house at Washington and Mason streets, now a municipal showplace as a result of a $60,000 refurbishing:

SAN FRANCISCO CABLE CAR SYSTEM
HAS BEEN DESIGNATED A
REGISTERED NATIONAL
HISTORIC LANDMARK
UNDER THE PROVISIONS OF THE
HISTORIC SITES ACT OF AUGUST 21, 1935
THIS SITE POSSESSES EXCEPTIONAL
VALUE IN COMMEMORATING OR
ILLUSTRATING THE HISTORY OF THE
UNITED STATES
U.S. DEPARTMENT OF THE INTERIOR
NATIONAL PARK SERVICE
1964

Officially, now, today accepts the presence of the cable car — evidence perhaps that man and machine do not always have to link forces grudgingly, nor do new plans have to be drawn every five years in the name of progress. The cable car conquers the hills of San Francisco as effectively as it did a century ago and with a style that extends inmeasurably beyond utility. As San Francisco Chronicle columnist Herb Caen put it, "What other mode of public transportation brings smiles to the faces of people who have to ride in it?"

BIBLIOGRAPHY

American Automobile Association, **Tour Book 1968-69.**

American Guide Series, **San Francisco, the Bay and Its Cities.**

Atherton, G., **My San Francisco** (including "The Ballad of the Hyde Street Grip," by G. Burgess), 1946.

Bailey, Almira, **Vignettes of San Francisco,** 1921.

Beebe, Lucius, **Cable Car Carnival,** 1951.

Bronson, William, **The Earth Shook, The Sky Burned,** 1959.

Cable Railway Co., **Cable Railway Company's System of Traction Railways for Cities and Towns,** 1881.

Caen, Herb, **The San Francisco Book,** 1948.

Dana, J., **The Man Who Built San Francisco,** 1936.

Dobie, Chas. C., **San Francisco, A Pageant,** 1936.

Enterprise Publishing Co., **The City of San Francisco and a Glimpse of California,** 1889.

Gilbert, G.K., **The San Francisco Earthquake & Fire,** Dept. of the Interior, U.S. Geological Survey, Bulletin No. 324, 1907.

Gilliam, Harold, **The Face of San Francisco,** 1960.

Hallidie, A.S., **Invention of the Cable Railroad System,** 1885.

Hawthorne, H., **Romantic Cities of California,** 1939.

Kahn, E.M., **Andrew S. Hallidie: A Tribute to a Pioneer California Industrialist,** 1953.

Kahn, E.M., **Cable Car Days in San Francisco,** 1940.

Kahn, E.M., **Cable Railway Propulsion,** 1952.

Lewis, O., **This Was San Francisco,** 1962.

Neville, A.R., **The Fantastic City,** 1932.

Meeker, **Harpers Weekly,** issue of Oct. 24, 1891.

Murray, Justin, **Cable Car Daze in San Francisco,** 1947.

O'Brien, Robert, "The Iowans and the Cable Car," **Riptides,** 1948.

Palmer, Phil and Mike, **The Cable Cars of San Francisco,** 1959 & 1963.

Parker, Frank, **Anatomy of the San Francisco Cable Car,** 1946.

Root, Henry, **Personal History and Reminiscence with Personal Opinion on Contemporary Events 1845-1921,** 1921.

Saunders, C.F., **Finding the Worth While in San Francisco,** 1916 & 1937.

"San Francisco Cable Cars," **Trains,** Nov. 1947.

Smith, J.B. and C.E., **A Treatise on Cable and Rope Traction, as Applied to Street and Other Railways,** 1887.

Thomas, Lynn, "A Cable Fable," **San Francisco,** July 1968.

Van, Melvin, **The Big Heart,** 1957.

Wagner, J.R., "Last of the Cable Cars," **Railroad,** 1945.

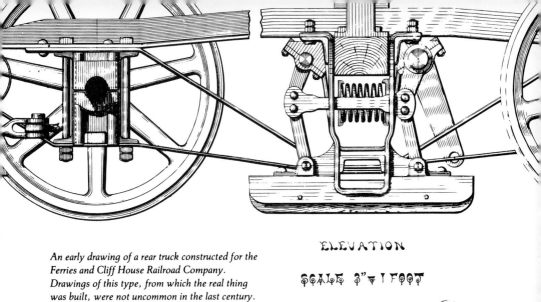

An early drawing of a rear truck constructed for the
Ferries and Cliff House Railroad Company.
Drawings of this type, from which the real thing
was built, were not uncommon in the last century.
Quite often such a drawing was something of an
unrecognized work of art. The original of the
drawing reproduced here is six times this size and
was done in ink on linen.

ELEVATION

SCALE 3" = 1 FOOT

PLAN

REAR TRUCK

FOR

FERRIES AND CLIFF HOUSE RY. CO.

MAHONY BROS.

BUILDERS

SAN FRANCISCO, CAL.

AS IT COULD BE

Our dependence on the automobile as primary transportation has transformed cities into efficient corridors filled with the presence of the car. San Francisco has attempted to soften this trend by the development of parks among the downtown buildings but automobiles still pervade the city. As pedestrians we're often dashing through the steel maelstrom hoping it won't pull us in. And those who live in San Francisco's neighborhoods are frequently assaulted by loud and smelly buses.

Yet the usual alternative to auto congestion is more public transport and that usually means buses. But nobody seems to get very excited about buses though perhaps the operation of open topped double-deckers might raise some eyebrows. Electric trolleycars bring a better response, probably because they're relatively benign street cruisers. But regardless of whether it's the trolley or bus, system designers usually emphasize speed and efficiency; a combination usually synonymous with sophisticated and expensive. Less tangible and more subjective values are rarely considered. For example, is the vehicle pleasant to operate? Is the ride enjoyable? Is overall freedom of action—including the movement of pedestrians, cyclists and cars—improved by public transportation? Is speed of such importance, at the expense of comprehensiveness, cost or comfort? What happens to property values before, during and after installation of different transport systems? Are these costly and, once installed, all pervasive machines what we really want and need or do they merely serve to alleviate one group of problems while simultaneously creating several more?

Typically the transport specialists are faced with riders living further and further away requiring faster and faster transportation to the central city. Yet as that transportation is provided it creates corridors of movement that by noise and pollution downgrade the community they pass through. In turn causing the residents to search for a new community—often in the suburbs. Obviously the transportation problem must be solved in a holistic manner, involving the whole community not just a small group of engineers. To that end we need alternatives that're not derived solely from an engineering mentality. Alternatives that solve many problems simultaneously.

Now the cable car is obviously not the answer to intercity transport problems, but as for the hilly inner-city a vehicle has not been devised that climbs hills quite as well as the cable car. Diesel buses do it loudly, trolley buses do it slowly and must have overhead wires. Both lack the cable car's grace, gliding as they do up and down the hills fitting intimately in scale with the Victorian language of the city's architecture. They feel, in speed and style, only a step away from walking.

Need everything invented in the 19th century be declared obsolete in a cold rush in the name of "progress?" Electric streetcars are undergoing a revival with new systems being planned or built in many cities. But pragmatists insist that cable cars are old-fashioned antiques to be relegated to museums. Why? Because they are not streamlined like an airplane and do not go faster than a speeding bullet? Yet ask any San Francisco visitor what they would like to do first and they will more than likely tell you: "See the bridges and ride the cable cars!" The fact remains that unlike practically any other form of public transportation the cable car actually draws crowds! To make our city livable can we learn to act with an awareness of all periods of mechanical history, just as we do in architectural history, rather than just the restrictive view of contemporary fashion?

Is it possible to expand the cable car system? Undoubtedly there is the demand to warrant it. Would it not be healthy for the city as a whole to have more visitors using cable cars instead of buses or their automobiles?

The cable car system is a division of the Municipal Railway of San Francisco; a division of the San Francisco Public Utilities Commission. According to their annual report (fiscal year 74-75) the cable car division carried 14,150,000 passengers and lost $3,027,000.

The Municipal Railway, financially aided under the Department of Transportation (DOT) Mass Transportation Act (MTA), is beginning to rebuild the cable car system's track, power plant sheaves, numerous cable cars and construct additional cable cars. Given the bureaucratic complexities of getting Federal aid as well as the money spent in the process, would it be wise to locally generate funds? Would that not encourage local, more direct, responsibility towards the whole transportation system?

Cable cars have been popular for decades. Why must San Francisco taxpayers as well as taxpayers at large pay for improvements when it's largely visitors who use the system for transport and recreation? The Santa Cruz roller coaster: 80 cents for a ride lasting approximately three minutes. Cable car: 25 cents for a ride that could last as long as 30 minutes! Would visitors object to a fare commensurate with the system's needs? Perhaps 50 cents, or 75? Assuming visitors pay the higher fare could regular riders have a card entitling them to ride at the 25 cent rate?

The cable car system has an annual employee turnover rate of almost 100 percent. Crowding and general hassling endured by the crews greatly contributes to the high attrition rate. The tension not only causes employees to leave but to abuse the equipment thereby passing their frustration on to maintenance personnel.

To reduce this costly turnover, increase care of equipment and consequently lower operating costs could gripmen and conductors organize into teams each responsible for a given cable car, including minor day to day maintenance? Consequently would they have a greater incentive to restrict the number of riders to a safe and manageable number? Could they collect fares and manage their income just as a small company would? A portion going to the larger organization for overall system maintenance? Perhaps the cable car division could be a private company chartered by the city? Residents could then purchase stock in the company entitling them to ride at the reduced rate. If the system had to support itself and to a greater degree than now, govern itself, it could be more responsive to the real demands placed upon it.

Assuming such an organization would result in a modestly profitable system could income then be used to expand the system?

Telegraph Hill, particularly the Coit Tower area, could benefit from a cable car line. Residents along Lombard Street — the principle access to Coit Tower — endure noisy and noxious cars driving up to circle around Coit Tower. A cable car line could be constructed up Union Street from Washington Square. At Montgomery the line could turn down to Greenwich Street where passengers could either depart for Coit Tower on foot or continue on Greenwich down the virtual cliff of Telegraph Hill (where the view of the bay would be fantastic!) to the waterfront. This would serve the Grant Street shops, the restaurants on top of Telegraph Hill and tie the northern waterfront — now undergoing a revival — into North Beach.

The Castro/Market street area out to Castro and 24th streets has undergone a rebirth. New shops, community services and restored Victorians attest to the community's vitality. That region, in the lee of Twin Peaks, is known for its high winds. A series of wind generators could be located around the slopes of Twin Peaks supplying electricity to a Castro Street powerhouse operating a cable car line over the Castro Street hill. Thereby tying together the Market/Castro community — with its new streetcar station — and the Castro/24th Street community.

The western end of the California Street cable line pleads for a destination. Why not continue the line from Van Ness Avenue out California to Fillmore, north to Sacramento Street and out to the Sacramento/Presidio Street shopping area? Its presence would encourage the development of business along Fillmore Street, connect a small shopping area with downtown and allow more commutors to use the California line to go downtown.

Union Street in the Marina district was renewed by private money, lots of it. In ten years a neighborhood shopping area evolved into singles bars, boutiques, and stores selling oddities you'd be pressed to find a use for. The boom has disrupted the neighborhood's character with traffic and parking becoming a major problem. Too many people with cars trying to fit in too small a space. Existing bus service — 45,41 lines — are perhaps adequate for the commute hours but later, when romance brings the crowds, most people drive. Buses just aren't very sexy. The Telegraph Hill line could be continued from Washington Square over Russian Hill and out Union to the Presidio. Parking on the shopping portion of Union Street could be limited allowing space for plazas, open markets and trees.

The cable car has remained virtually unchanged despite our obvious technological advances since 1873. Considering how well the system continues despite its antiquated machinery perhaps it would be best to leave most of it alone.

But there are devices that could improve the system's workings and lower maintenance costs. Already the Muni is installing an electronic cable monitering device to minimize the chance of costly accidents. Beyond that they are studying the possibility of using roller bearings and automatic lubricating devices on the various cable guidance mechanisms. Undoubtedly these are much needed improvements but need the effort stop there?

A major track reconstruction project is already planned. Instead of rebuilding the existing could a precast concrete tie structure replace the existing steel structure, particularly on Powell, Hyde Street hills? An open, lattice-like structure permitting planting of pollution resistant vines and shrubs. The addition of the greenery would be welcome; for visually breaking otherwise dull pavement and increasing oxygen in the atmosphere. The plants and soil would absorb most of the cable car's noise while insuring that autos could not trespass on the right of way.

Most of the cabinetmaking involved in constructing a cable car represents a peak in 19th century coachbuilding craft. Cable cars built in the past ten years demonstrate the abilities of the few craftsmen retaining the art. It would be wise to insure knowledge of these crafts remain in order to maintain contact with the roots of contemporary technology. Particularly because our present situation seems to demand a partial return to simpler, smaller-scale and more human technology.

Through the cable car division or a local university could there be a college of antiquated technology? Classes in metal, wood crafts and the design philosophy of earlier periods, particularly the 19th century?

There is no reason why new cable cars could not be constructed. Machines that respectfully update the spirit and techniques of the originals. After all, we have not changed much in size and shape and the form of the cable car is still an accurate reflection of our physical needs. A few interesting and potentially profitable possibilities:

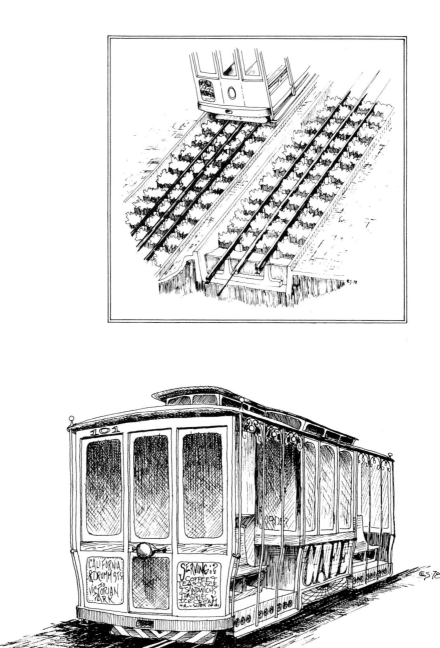

A rolling sandwich and refreshment car leased out by the cable car division as a private concession. Riders could board downtown, ride up over Nob Hill on the California line, buy lunch on the way, get off at the top of the hill, have lunch in the park and ride another car downtown. Or one could stay aboard and eat lunch with a constantly changing view of the city. On warm evenings hot drinks could be served to people out on the town.

An open-sided car would be very useful for touring convention groups in addition to normal service. Rented on an hourly basis, including a crew doubling as guides, the car could tour the cable lines and with sidings at turntables and along the route visitors could disembark on neighborhood walking tours.

The Union Street and outer California/Sacramento Streets routes would require powerhouses. They needn't be dull industrial facilities or semi-museums like the existing powerhouse. They could be urban sculpture with large glass panels allowing pedestrians to view the spinning sheaves, a cafe integrated within and a gallery arrangement where cable cars are repaired allowing college of antiquated technology classes to observe real work being done.

There would undoubtedly be many problems in expanding the cable car system. Technical problems notwithstanding there are potentially numerous difficulties with political groups, unions and citizens. There is also understandable concern for the machine's efficiency. It takes a large staff to operate the existing cable system and labor is expensive, as are the many specially made parts. But the mechanical and operating characteristics of the system reflect the inefficiency of the bureaucratic style that governs it. Civil service positions are notoriously soft and there is little incentive to make things work smoothly, last long and cost less. For example, there is little incentive to make design changes allowing off-the-shelf parts needing no special machining. Therefore it is difficult if not impossible to compare costs with bus or streetcar operations (which also lose money) including the real costs of both: maintaining streets versus tracks, energy cost per passenger carried (including energy used to make the materials and build the vehicle), and overall maintenance cost.

Technology is the science of tools we use to serve ourselves. Can we use our technology to design environments that're healthy for all life? Is there any objective that is more important?

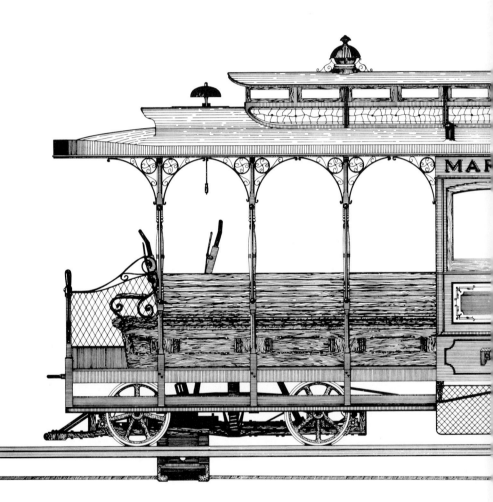